ARDENS SED VIRENS

BLACKMOUTH & DISSENTER

John M. Barkley

The White Row Press

BLACKMOUTH & DISSENTER

John M. Barkley

The White Row Press

First published 1991 by
The White Row Press
135 Cumberland Road
Dundonald, Belfast BT16 0BB

Cover: the Reverend Professor John Monteith Barkley M.A., B.D., Ph.D., D.D., in
the library of Union Theological College, Belfast; Pope John Paul II meets Dr.
Barkley, 1979; endpapers: the original 'burning bush' of 1842.

The publishers gratefully acknowledge the financial assistance of the Presbyterian
Association in the publication of this book.

British Library Cataloguing In Publication Data

Barkley, John M. (John Monteith)
Blackmouth and dissenter — the autobiography of John Barkley.
1. Presbyterian churches 2. Northern Ireland
I. Title
285. 2416

ISBN 1 870132 45 9 (cloth)

Typeset by Island Publications, Belfast
Printed by the Universities Press Ltd., Belfast

Blackmouth & Dissenter

Preface		8
1.	In my father's house	13
2.	By Derry's walls	32
3.	The Meetinghouse at the Cross	49
4.	Across the borders	64
5.	Taking stands: the call to Cooke	83
6.	A broader horizon	102
7.	Principal Barkley	120
8.	Service and dissent	135
9.	Progressus ex variis frustrationibus!	151
10.	Opening the field	172
Appendix A: reasons for dissent		181
Appendix B: complete bibliography		184
Chronology		189
Abbreviations		190

Maps

Malin, Co. Donegal, c. 1913	12
Drumreagh, Co. Antrim, c. 1935	50
Cooke Centenary, Belfast	82
Ireland, showing some of the places mentioned in the text	180

Preface

Frequently prefaces are not read. They should be, if for no other reason than that they are generally written last. I had no intention of writing this book but, having agreed to do so, many faces have come floating into the mirror of memory. Some of them are smiling, others have tears of gladness shining in their eyes. Some are solemn, and others are lined with care and grief. Some come from childhood, others from college days. Some are from areas where I lived, others from lands I visited. Many appear in these pages, others cannot because of reasons of space or confidentiality.

In many ways, this is no more than the story of a boy growing up in home, community and church in Ireland, who in his early teens often fell asleep to the sound of shooting between the B Specials and the IRA, heard whispered talk (so that he would not hear) when his father was sent for because someone had been murdered, kidnapped or intimidated. He still remembers vividly, when he was about ten, sitting with a gun about three inches from his head in James Simpson's Model T, while his father and James were held up.

He grew up and God called him to be a minister of the Gospel. Periodically, throughout his life he has known good Christian men shot, innocent women and children bereaved and maimed, homes and property destroyed. He has known some to end their earthly life being gathered on a shovel into a plastic bag. Behind his life, therefore, is a back-cloth of hate, murder and atrocity, of distortion, misrepresentation and injustice. Should these pages be simply a narrative of facts? Is a minister of the Gospel simply called to be 'a nice man', or should he believe in and witness to certain things?

I have lived in the peaceful and rugged countryside of Inishowen, in the border-wrecked town of Aughnacloy, and the uneasy trinity of Derry, Waterside and Bogside. I received my university education in Derry, Dublin and Belfast and have ministered in North Antrim, Co. Monaghan, and Belfast. May this be reduced to nothing more than narrative? Surely not. Space must be made for some of what I, as a Christian minister, believe. What I have written is not worth reading, unless behind the back-cloth of hate there is to be seen the hope which flows from belief in the grace of God in Christ.

There was a time in Ireland when all held presbyterianism to pay more than lip-service to 'human rights' and 'common sense' *per se*. Its social radicalism demanded justice for all, that 'every species of persecution for religious opinions be done away', and that 'intolerance of every kind may be trodden underfoot'. Presbyterians were respected for their integrity and independence even though they were disparagingly referred to as 'dissenters' and 'blackmouths'. From this I take my title. These terms need clarification.

The term dissenter, like the word 'protestant', is positive, not negative. It means to 'witness to'. In Europe, there developed the system of one sovereign and one form of church-life within which no dissent was allowed. Germany was divided into Roman Catholic and Lutheran areas, the religion of each being determined by the religion of the prince. This really meant 'conform or emigrate'.

In England each change in the reigns of Henry VIII, Edward VI, Mary, and Elizabeth was intended to embrace all citizens, and the efforts to repress dissent continued for almost two centuries. It is not necessary to continue the story, or relate how Ireland became involved through the actions of Popes Adrian IV and Alexander III, the Synod of Cashel, and the grant of Pope Innocent III to King John and his successors. Suffice it to say, that the dissenting aim was to follow Scripture and the "best Reformed Churches", "to give life a sense of value", to be "independent", and "to reduce politics and the whole of life to ethical standards". These are still worthy aims and part of my inheritance as a presbyterian. Without 'refusing light from any quarter', as a member I have a responsibility to the Presbyterian Church in Ireland, but should I find anything therein to be at variance with presbyterianism's calling to be a witness to the mind and spirit of Christ, dissent is necessary.

It must be constructive dissent. It has nothing to do with quibblers.

Presbyterians were disparagingly referred to as blackmouths in Ireland in the final two decades of the eighteenth century. That they were so-called because their mouths were stained black by eating blaeberries when forced to flee as fugitives during the Killing Times in Scotland is a myth and completely false. There is no evidence for such a use in any part of Scotland.

The term is Irish in origin and its connotation is political. It refers to those whose sympathies lay with the ideals of social polity and human rights in the American and French Revolutions. Eventually the epithet came to be applied to the whole presbyterian community. From around 1780 onwards:

an ancient term of forthright abuse was seized by a section of the ascendency party, and flung at a body of people whom it had often reviled, and many of whom were implicated in rebellious projects, and several of whom were ringleaders in the Rebellion itself.

The aim of the Blackmouths was to establish unity and brotherhood among all the people of Ireland, to achieve "parliamentary reform by constitutional means", and to include "Irishmen of every religious persuasion" in the reform so that it may be "efficacious and just". In its origins there was no approval of the use of force.

The social influence of presbyterianism appears to have declined in recent years with the unchallenged and unrebuked growth of sectarianism. When class-hatred is inflamed with religious fanaticism abstract statements are futile. The radical stand of the Blackmouths against a despotic and sectarian State is still a worthy cause:

If from pressure from vested interests (religious or secular) the State pursues a policy involving injustice or a plain denial of equal fellowship, the Church which silently acquiesces is rightly discredited.

I often wonder how far the Presbyterian Church in Ireland and myself as a member of it have been faithful to these elements of our presbyterian past.

This book was written at the request of friends. In it, I have tried to be objective and though it has been necessary to refer to some regrettable events my hope is that it will contribute to establishing more Christian inter-church and community relations in Ireland. Writing completely from memory, to avoid inaccuracies I have had to ask many people for help. For their assistance in this way, I thank Mrs June Baird, Mrs Maureen Cousley, Mrs Dorothy Dunlop, Mrs Jean Hanna, Mrs Daphne Holmes-Greer and Mrs Doreen McDowell, Revs S.J. Campbell, Richard C. Graham, Walter Herron, John Lappin, Charles McKeag, Ian H. Marshall and Robin Morton.

In particular, I thank Miss Margaret Ritchie for typing my manuscript, Mr Paddy Donnelly for reading the first draft, Dr. Damian Smyth for helping to prepare the final text, and the Rev. K. Compton for permission to quote from her poem, *Christchild.*

None of the above are in the slightest way responsible for any opinion expressed in the book — the buck, if there is any, stops with me.

Finally, I thank the Presbyterian Association, Dublin, for its generous contribution towards the cost of publication and also two friends who wish to remain anonymous.

John M. Barkley
St. Patrick's Day, 1991

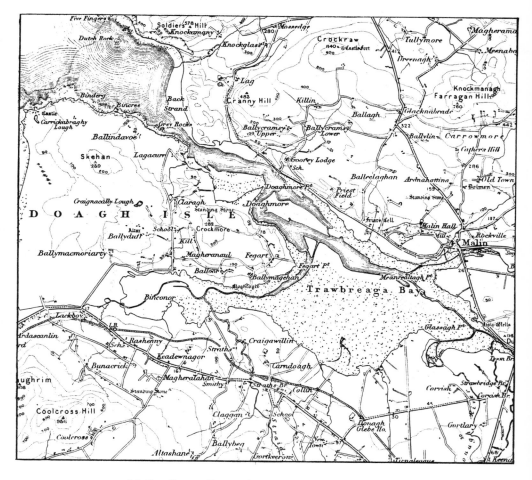

Malin, County Donegal, as it was during John Barkley's boyhood.
The Meetinghouse was near the bar of the bay, just beyond Goorey School.

1 In my father's house

Like my father and grandfather before me, I grew up within Irish presbyterianism. Indeed, this is an understatement. I was steeped in it, nursed and nurtured in it, to the point where I cannot be abstracted from it or it from me. For me, this presbyterianism was not, as one too often sees it characterised, a dry and arid dust, it was a rich, congenial soil in which to grow.

I do not remember my paternal grandmother, but I do remember my grandfather — John Barkley, farmer, of Glenhue, Ahoghill, Co Antrim. He died in his one-hundredth year, having been given twenty-four hours to live before I was born. My father had in his study the famous picture of John Knox with his long flowing beard which used to adorn manses and session-rooms. As a child, I always referred to it as grandfather, and indeed it was a striking likeness. When staying there he would take me for a walk round the farm. I loved this, especially when our way led by the flush, along the river, through the garden-orchard, and the fields beyond. I do not remember much of what he said, but I do recall his saying:

"Today we will follow the path I took every morning when my father sent me out to examine the potatoes during the famine to see if the blight had come".

The famine was clearly a watershed in his life: it was said that if he saw a potato lying by the roadside, he would pick it up and bring it home in his pocket.

My grandfather was a Christian man, straight and honest, independent and stubborn — that is, he had most of the characteristics of his fellow presbyterians. Each week when *The Witness,* the presbyterian newspaper, arrived he sat down and read it from beginning to end.

Politically, grandfather was a Liberal and a Home Ruler and had little time for Orange-Toryism. Indeed, when he heard that I had gone to see an Orange procession at Ewart's cross, he gave me a hiding, even though I was then quite a lump of a boy. He knew that the earliest Lodges were constituted under the bishop's mitre of the Ascendancy, and he did not forget it.

He would not let coal into the house, where all cooking was done over a turf-fire on the hanging griddle, the big black pots, oven and kettle. There was one thing for which I never quite forgave my uncles and aunts. My grandfather died on a Tuesday and was buried on Friday and they had a coal stove installed on the Wednesday or Thursday. To me, they would have honoured their father's memory far more truly had they been prepared to wait a week before doing so. Anyway, Aunt Aggie's wonderful soda farls never tasted quite the same again.

My father, Robert James Barkley, was the second son and middle child of the family of seven. Samuel, my father's elder brother, was a carpenter and Johnny, a younger, farmed. Aggie was the cook (and a good one), Martha and Annie were dress-makers, and Meg worked on the farm (I liked her but always thought she was a slave to the other three). Somewhere along the line the family had joined Trinity, Ahoghill, and it was there I was taken to church if I stayed the week-end. They were very 'religious' and Glenhue was a regular centre for cottage meetings. While acknowledging their absolute sincerity, their religion differed from that in which I had been nourished. I was not "a child of God" but "a heathen needing conversion". The limits to which their religion extended may be seen in the fact that uncle Tom found it necessary to resign as Sunday-School superintendent because, with permission having been given by the Session for the playing of badminton, the floor of the hall had been marked out in courts and "the white lines were a sign that the devil was present". At the same time, they were good and sincere people who loved me very much. I never had the honour of preaching in Trinity, Ahoghill.

The Jacksons and the Taylors neighboured Glenhue. In the latter Andrew, pronounced 'Anra', lived with his sister. He belonged to First Ahoghill. He was not Gospel-greedy. Being a presbyterian, he knew he had a soul, but believed it was in God's keeping so he did not worry too much about it. God could be trusted and depended upon. One day, when he was cutting down a hedge with an slasher along came a man in a hard hat, black coat, striped trousers, and cloth shoes and started into Anra about his soul. Anra went on with his work and the man duly upbraided him for not listening. At that Anra, resting the slasher on the ground and with his elbow leaning on the shaft, said:

"I'll stop an' listen t'ye, if ye'll answer wan question.What's the chief end o' man?"

The man started into a long answer, but before he had gone very far Anra declared:

"Man's chief end is to glorify God and enjoy him forever".

The man expressed his admiration, to which Anra said:

"Aye, an' I ha' a wee book in the house there wi' a hunyerd and seven just as good. I holt ye ye'r nae presbyterian, but one o' them dippers frae the tent".

The man at once demanded to know what was wrong with being a dipper.

"Jest wan thing. When ye put them un'er the water ye let them up owre soon".

While my aunts raged, I learned from Anra that it isn't wise to tackle people without knowing what you are up against. The likes of Anra is no dozer and can see through one without much difficulty. There is at least one Anra in every congregation. Thank God.

My mother was Mary Darcus Monteith, daughter of John Monteith, farmer, Killygordon, Castlefin, Co Donegal. Her mother, Mary Darcus, was a Huguenot. I never knew either of my maternal grandparents, but certain events told by my mother about her father established a real kinship. He was an elder in Donoughmore congregation. In a former day, some Roman Catholics made a presbyterian executor when drawing up their wills. This was said to be for two reasons. They knew that because of their reputation for honesty the details of the will would be carried out faithfully; and they knew that details regarding their finances would not be disclosed to anyone. A Roman Catholic neighbour had left my grandfather as executor in the year 1859 and, as he went into Castlefin to attend the Revival meetings, he sometimes called in when passing to see how the widow and orphans were getting along, and every night, as he was leaving, she sprinkled him with holy water "so that he wouldn't be converted because he was an upright man". It is what a man is, not what he professes, which is the important thing in life.

Another incident my mother related concerned the Rev. Robert Smyth of Donoughmore. He was a 'gun of the Gospel' as a preacher and was worshipped by all the people, but he had a 'little weakness'. Everyone knew about it but, because of his kindness and devotion, no-one ever spoke ill of him. My grandfather's part in this was that on occasion on a Saturday night he brought Mr Smyth home from Castlefin in his wheel-barrow, to enable him to get his sermon ready for Sunday. While, without question, Mr Smyth would have been better off had he been a tee-totaller, my grandfather's behaviour showed me the necessity of tolerance.

My mother had a brother, John Monteith, after whom I was called. He was kind and generous. Everybody liked and trusted him. Though lacking schooling, he was well read and, though I do not know whether or not his mother being a Huguenot had anything to do with it, he was extremely knowledgeable about French history. When he died his library contained over four hundred books on Napoleon and the French Revolution. He used to say, when started,

"There's nothing quite like the blue, the white, the red".

He also had a remarkable gift, namely, that he could read a column of the *Tele* over once, hand the paper to you, and repeat it word for word. He claimed to be a fisherman. Indeed, when he died, there were twenty-six rods to be disposed of. However, I never quite believed this because I am certain I never heard him tell a story about 'the one that got away'. Having fished myself, I regard this as very peculiar — all my big ones got away.

My parents were poor. My father's stipend in Malin was £30 a year, paid annually in arrears. Christmas brought a pair of socks or jumper knitted by my mother, a few sweets, an orange, and a half-crown which had to find its way into the mission box before lunchtime. Uncle John did not always come for Christmas, but when he did there was always something for my sister and myself. We liked him because he was jolly, but at times he could be very serious as when he told the pair of us how his father, a widower, was put out of his farm rather than leave the Presbyterian Church. He had walked my mother and her young brother from Donegal to Belfast to find work.

Everybody knew him as 'John' and, so far as I know, I never had a nickname either. One morning when I was in Belfast studying for the ministry, a telegram addressed to my parents arrived at Claremont Manse: "John died in RVH this morning". The immediate thought was that I had been hurt playing rugby. My mother collapsed on the stairs and, though in his poor state of health it was enough to kill him, my father got up and phoned the RVH. They assured him that no John Barkley had died there, so he asked "Who did die?" They read the names and when they came to 'John Monteith' he said "I know who it is now". After this, he had to console my mother on the death of her only brother but, in a sense, the shock was eased because I was safe and well. While I knew my parents loved me and cared for me, this event brought it home to me with a force I had never known before.

My father was a good student but lack of money meant that he had few opportunities to study. He was a city missionary but, when the Mission became a company under the Company Act of 1907, he became a student for the Ministry of the Presbyterian Church in Ireland, attending Magee College, Derry, and New College, Edinburgh. In 1910, he entered his final year in Assembly's College, Belfast. As his Arts course fell in the years following the Irish Universities Act (1908) and before the agreement between Magee and Trinity College Dublin, my father graduated GAMC (Graduate of Arts Magee College). Having no university degree, he studied, teaching himself, and obtained the degree of Bachelor of Divinity of the Presbyterian Theological Faculty, Ireland, in 1916. He was ordained by the Presbytery of Derry in Malin on 20 February,1913. Those were the days when an ordination was an ordination — the Service being followed by a dinner with a soirée in the evening. Malin being a far northern outpost, there were no professional artistes for the programme, so the ministers, who stayed for the evening, sang songs, told stories, recited poems and entertained the assembled multitude. Thank goodness, ordinations were still a great occasion in 1935 when I too was ordained.

The lack of distinguished artistes was no reflection on the congregation. It was geographic. When my father went to a presbytery meeting in Derry, he rose at 5.30 a.m., left the manse at 6.30, cycled nine miles to Carndonagh and caught the Lough Swilly train, arriving in Derry about 10.30. The return journey ended in walking up the manse avenue about 11.30 p.m. Presbytery needed to be worth going to in those days. Indeed, one of my father's predecessors was fined for non-attendance.

Although I was born in Belfast, all my earliest memories of life are of Malin — Church, Goorey National School, playing tig with my sister, horses, dulse, sand dunes, loanin's, the smell of spring soil, Willie Tom Colhoun, Rab of Bellelaghan, Molly of Priestfield, Henry Boggs, the Davises, Doagh Island, Inistrahull, the roaring of the bar, Trawbreaga Bay, Quigley's bull, Lagg Chapel, Mr Lamont, school-master in Keenagh, (who threw his arms around me on the floor of the Assembly Hall as if I was his own son on my appointment as a professor); and washing through and around it all, the great current of Irish presbyterianism. May God forgive me should I ever forget my roots with the Boggs, Fultons, Sterritts, Hendersons, Colhouns and Davises of Malin.

It was in Malin that I first attended church. Shortly before my sister was born, I was proving somewhat of a nuisance so, to give my mother peace, my father took me by the hand and gave me over to Willie Tom to sit with him. I have been given to understand that I was quite well behaved, but did not think very much of my father's sermon as I asked for my penny back when the service was over. My father later ministered in Aughnacloy (1917-26) and in Loanends (1926-29), County Antrim, and Claremont, Derry (1929-44).

I recall three small but significant things that may give you a flavour of life in Malin. When my sister Alison was born, my mother was very ill, and every Sunday Father Doherty prayed for her at mass. I remember my father speaking of this in appreciative terms. Then there was the Ancient Order of Hibernians. They may not have paraded every year past the manse, but sometimes they did. This was noteworthy for the fact that when they came to the manse march-ditch, the band stopped playing until it left the townland of

Ballymagroarty. The same practice was followed at the Meetinghouse.

While it did not mean anything to me then, I remember favourable comment on this behaviour. There was respect for those of a different viewpoint.

The same could be said of Henry Boggs and his workmen. Henry was a presbyterian and they were Roman Catholics. He had the salmon fishing rights on Trawbreaga Bay and caught dabs and so on, as well as the salmon. So the fishermen got fish on Sunday, Monday, Tuesday, Wednesday, Thursday, roast beef on Friday and fish again on Saturday. Unlike today there were no accusations of discriminatioon or sectarianism. All knew the butcher's van only came round from Carndonagh on a Friday.

Henry was an interesting character. He wouldn't handle paper money, only sovereigns. He loved his cows so much that he had a door from the bedroom into the byre in case one was calving or sick. When my father was leaving Malin, Henry said to him:

"Mr Barkley, I'd rather one of my cows had died than you're leaving us".

My father always held that it was one of the highest tributes he had ever been paid.

To go to Malin one leaves Derry, skirting the shores of Lough Foyle, and heads for Culmore and Muff, for Moville and Inishowen Head but, a few miles short of Moville at Quigley's Point, one turns left up into the mountain passes through Glen Tougher, for Carndonagh. About three miles further on, one comes to the bridges over Trawbreaga Bay and Malin Town and, following the shoreline about three miles further, one comes to Goorey rocks and the road which formerly led to the National School and passes Davis's, then the road ends and one steps on to the foreshore. There, sitting on the sand is Malin Meetinghouse, round which the Atlantic sweeps in twice a day. At this point, too, standing in the sandhills, is Lagg Chapel. There they stand, a living memorial to the days when presbyterians and Roman Catholics were treated as religious and social outcasts.

Not surprisingly, given the tides, Malin Meetinghouse had no graveyard of its own. This was true until well after my father's time, when a main country road was built. I later learned that three of the first four presbyterian ministers of Malin were buried in the Catholic graveyard at Lagg. Not only that, some years ago, when I went to search for the three graves I found that the original Boggs, Hendersons, Colhouns and so on, had also been buried there. Theological differences had not destroyed social relationships. Today, things are greatly changed — the county road runs between the Meetinghouse and the sea, Goorey National School has been turned into a summer residence and presbyterians no longer bury their dead in Lagg having a kirk-yard of their own.

The congregation consisted of a school-teacher, the post-mistress and some sixty farming families. Life was hard. The daily fare was porridge, sometimes bacon and eggs, home-made bread, with potatoes and salt. Meat was scarce but a pig would be killed and cured for the winter. They were a sober people but it was possible (if one knew where) to get a taste of the 'craitur'. They knew all their neighbours worshipped in Lagg, and that they themselves worshipped in the Meetinghouse, but they lived together, and were devout, conservative and tolerant in their ways. They reverenced Scripture and *The Shorter Catechism,* and because there was no wireless, the community was centred on the church and the fair at Carndonagh.

Aughnacloy brought me face to face with issues hitherto unknown to me: sectarianism and community division. It was a microcosm of the tragedy of Irish history. There were three schools — the Pound (RC), Glack (Anglican) and Caledon Street (presbyterian). It was here, by the merest chance, that I had contact with Ken Maginnis' father. He was an Anglican and went to Glack, so I only met him if I needed something from his grandfather's tailor shop. We were well and truly segregated. Add to this the fact that the Manse was about a mile out of town, and that on good days I was usually given work to do in the garden — meaning that I had little contact with other children outside school. At this period, Ireland was partitioned and I remember the Cameronians being billeted in the McIlwaine Presbyterian Church Hall and parading to church. I remember my father being called out on emergency pastoral visits (which were never discussed in front of the children). I remember the kidnappings and rumours and falling asleep night after night to the rattle of gunfire between the IRA and the B Specials.

Originally, Aughnacloy had only the Ulster Bank, then along came the Belfast, and at a later date the Northern. Such financial edifices gave the town the appearance of prosperity but it was only an appearance. The border runs within a quarter-mile of the town. This was disastrous as it served large tracts of Co. Monaghan. Business after business left the town to go to Larne, Ballymena and elsewhere. The congregation in Aughnacloy consisted of a dozen businesses (reduced to five) and forty farmers. The Farming life was a harsh one. Business melted away. People lived in fear of arson and assassination. Blood was shed.

Another revelation was what passed for inter-church relations, at least so far as the Protestant churches were concerned. The Anglicans continued to act as if they were the Establishment. Presbyterians behaved as if they were still living in the eighteenth century. Both of them scorned the Methodists. Inter-church relations never arose except in relation to the Orange service on the first Sunday of July, traditionally held in the Anglican and Presbyterian Churches in alternate years. My father refused to participate unless he was given a part in the service which, in accordance with Anglican theology, recognised the validity of Presbyterian Ordination. Needless to say, this created great tension every time it came up. Sadly, Aughnacloy had never heard of ecumenism.

Being Christians and having received the gift of a child, one of the first responsibilities of my parents was to have him baptised. He was born within the Covenant and so was entitled to all its privileges, especially to have it declared unto him that God loved him before he was able to love God. On the day, my mother took me to church on a jaunting car, and all went well until, on the return journey, the horse shied and deposited my mother and myself in the ditch.

Neither of us was hurt, though some people like to assure me I have never recovered from it.

Baptism is a sacrament of the Gospel effectual through the blessing of Christ. There are those today who repudiate their baptism. This I believe to be due to a lack of understanding, in that baptism is not founded simply on a text but on the nature and character of God as revealed by Jesus Christ, placing one within God's earthly family. I did not grasp the revolutionary impact of this until many years had passed.

I was brought up in an era when the minister's child had to excel

Caesar's wife in every virtue. This is what the members of the congregation expected. The grocer's son might rob an orchard, but not the minister's; anyone's motorbike might kill a hen without any problem but, should it happen to the minister's son, he had to get rid of it. Indeed, for a minor offence, it was possible for the minister to be informed that the claimant would pay no more stipend and I received quite a roasting on one such occasion. This certainly moulded 'who' and 'what' I am — I have no time for tale-bearers. I despise them. I learned to treat with contempt all glib accusations against myself; and if made against anyone to whom I owe a loyalty, I must be in the van in their defence. Sadly, while never much given to criminal wickedness, I found there were too many people prepared to rehearse my slightest misdemeanour.

This had another side. The schoolmaster was a decent man but he had one weakness — he was incapable of finding the true culprit when a misdemeanour occurred. Of course, he had to have a culprit. If he caned an innocent child, his or her mother or father was down at the school next day. So, if the real culprit could not be identified, one of two boys, whose parents believed that if the master caned you, you must have been guilty, were caned daily for things that they had not done.

I was one of them. The other was an orphan. While not approving of their doctrine of the inerrancy of school discipline, I had had my parents. My pal had lost his father, injustice had led him to reject his mother's discipline and the last I heard of him, in 1985, he had spent years in prison. This experience helped to make me rebellious against authority, despising those who sought to exercise authority solely because of office or for self-advancement.

Now, how can I tell about my father — when no words of mine can adequately pay tribute to him?

He was a good man, very upright in his dealing with all men. He had his views on various subjects. My father was a militant tee-totaller. I mention this because, not infrequently, Temperance Sunday provided merriment for my mother and myself. The organist in Claremont worked in a distillery and often played as the voluntary during the offering the tune Whiskey Johnny. The reason for our amusement was that my father was tone-deaf: he never knew what was being played.

Father was a fairly strict Sabbatarian — shoes were cleaned and floors swept on Saturday evening. There was no playing games or weekday frivolities, no *Children's Newspaper,* only the Bible or *Scots Worthies.* My reaction to this as a child can be summed up in a remark I made to my sister on one occasion, when sabbatically fed-up: "Come on down to the kitchen — it may not be the Sabbath there".

Sunday meant going to church, reading holy books, going to church and, as Pepys said, "so to bed". In spite of this, I did not dislike Sunday School and owe much to my teachers, Tommy Henderson and, especially, Jim Kyle. It was Jim who pointed out to me that Christ's humiliation consist*ed.* It was in the past whereas his exultation consist*eth:* it is on-going. When I asked how God could forgive me as I forgave others for I had only been sinned against a few times but had often sinned myself, I remember Jim explaining that the petition referred to 'quality' not 'quantity. It was the quality of the forgiveness that mattered. Indeed, it was Jim who first related this petition to 'sin' as he used this term to explain 'debts' and 'trespasses'. While most of his words are forgotten, the impact of his character remains.

My father was a very fair and honest man. I remember his counsel: "John, remember, in any case of difficulty, it is far better that a guilty man gets off than an innocent man ever be found guilty". This is how he approached problems and I only hope I have lived up to it. Indeed, it was this very saying which made me support inserting in the 1980 edition of *The Code:*

Every court, congregation and member of the Presbyterian Church in Ireland is governed and protected by this Code. People have rights.

My father was interested in amateur sport but absolutely opposed professionalism. Hence, going to Brandywell to support Derry City created problems. So, also, did going to the cinema. He did not so much object to the films as to the many-times married actors and actresses. Of course, I was of a different age group but an age gap was never allowed to develop. He knew I went; I knew he knew I went. There was nothing behind-back. There was toleration with the occasional comment to make sure we didn't get our lines crossed. On the other hand, the car was mine to ferry half the rugby team to Limavady or Strabane, or half the hockey team to Ballybofey or

Raphoe.

He was a good preacher and the whole Service was carefully prepared. His sermons were stimulating if one was prepared to think, though they were perhaps a bit longer than is the rule today. They were not essays but, instead, applied evangelical truth to daily life. His ministry in prayer was devotional and real. He was nervous and tense within himself in the pulpit, but one would not have noticed this until his serious illness. I remember his saying to me: "John, coming to Claremont had one great advantage. I no longer have to go the vestry door five or six times before I can open it. Now, James Maconaghie comes and I have to follow".

I had myself to face the same harsh fact of walking out to face a congregation, and this common experience was one of the strongest bonds between us.

A particular mark of my father was his pastoral fidelity. I remember many instances of this — when James Simpson was kidnapped by the IRA and the mail was stolen and the day Thomas Hadden, the auctioneer, and Ankatell Moutry were abducted by the same faction.

Then there was the day I will never forget. About a year and a half after going to Claremont my father had 'flu and had been in bed for five or six days. A death occurred in the congregation. My father rose from his sick-bed and conducted the funeral, the snow lying five inches deep in the City Cemetery. When he returned, breathing very heavily, he sat down at the fire and, tapping his chest, he said: "John, my chest feels like a block of wood". He continued to cough, followed after some time by a violent-red stream of blood. I'll never forget it. I was scared stiff.

My father had acute bronchitis. However his doctor prescribed medicines to make him cough, and I am convinced that, had this man not himself fallen ill and stopped practicing, my father would not have survived. His new doctor was shocked by what he found, and ordered complete rest and an immediate three-month holiday in the south of England. My father was very weak and my mother took him to Sidmouth in Devon. I don't remember anything much about the twice-weekly letters from my mother, but it is funny what sticks in one's mind — one of them described them eating strawberries and cream in November. I was left to look after things with my sister. Of course, as a child, I had learnt to sweep floors, wash dishes and cook a little, so the pair of us got through. When my father returned, he was a frail, broken man — coughing, spitting blood, feeling faint, until he died on 2 March, 1944. During that sixteen years, one man in particular stood by my father and mother. He drove my father to church and home again. He walked home with him from Session meetings. He would joke with my mother about delivering him safely. He was a real pillar of strength to her. It is important that I should acknowledge the goodness of John McCarter.

There was more to my father's illness than this. There was no National Health Service, so every penny had to go on buying steak to squeeze the blood out of it, eggs and special medicine to keep my father alive. He could not retire. My mother was, to all intents and purposes, destitute, with two children attending Magee University College. At this time, the choice for me was to win a scholarship or not be back at College the following year. I must express my gratitude to the ministers of the Derry presbytery for giving me supplies regularly after I entered my first theological year.

My father's illness also affected my approach to study. In Magee, there were special scholarship examinations in September. The college course consisted of classes, with examinations at the end of the year. In the latter, prizes were only given to the first two in each subject and they were worth £2 and £1. In September, on the other hand, one could get £35 or £30 which kept you for a year in those days. Along with the situation arising from my father's illness, during the session my one aim was to achieve 40 per cent and to work during the summer for a scholarship. This meant that during term-time there was plenty of time for rugby, hockey, soccer and other sporting activities.

After my experiences in Caledon Street Public Elementary School in Aughnacloy, my response to education was to be interested in subjects where I liked the teacher and not to be interested where I did not. However, when I was sixteen, my whole outlook changed — without any loss of interest in maths, physics and chemistry which had been my strengths. I got a new teacher in English and became fascinated with English literature. Before I was nineteen, I had read most of Dickens, Walter Scott, Mrs Gaskell, George Eliot and so on — not to mention Shakespeare, Wordsworth, Keats, Shelley, Tennyson and Browning. I had found a whole new world.

Also, Miss Dora Suffern, a school-teacher and member of the Loanends congregation, introduced me to Jean Valjean when she gave me a present of Victor Hugo's *Les Misérables* on my sixteenth birthday. Jean and Sydney Carton became my favourite characters and I wished I could be like them. I had entered into the world of romance, terror, tragedy and integrity. At this time, too, I learned something more: the teacher's task is not to teach so much as to inspire one to love the subject. I discovered that, given this love, one taught oneself. This was to prove very significant for me as a postgraduate student.

My father was a farmer's son and, had he remained on the farm, he would have prospered because he had green fingers. Everything he planted grew. At Malin, he planted all the trees at the Manse. At Aughnacloy, the avenue was one hundred and fifty yards long and had to be scuffled twice a year. There were two orchards. The first of August each year saw a call for the scythe to cut the nettles so that the windfalls would not be lost. At the front was a sloping lawn filled with shrubs — lupins, lilacs, daphne museum, broom — with flower-beds full of sweet william, daffodils, crocuses, pansies, tulips, chrysanthemum; and in front of that a tennis-court to be cut twice a week in the summer and a rock garden round three sides of it. In the back garden, there were apples, plums, pears, black and red currants, strawberries, raspberries, cabbages, cauliflower, potatoes, beet, peas and beans, gooseberries, vegetable marrows, leeks and onions, carrots and parsnips. These my father worked by himself with two helpers — my sister and myself. The weather, looking back, appears to have been much better than now, for all I can remember is every day after school being turned to some task in the garden or to cut the grass. I learned a lot about feeding marrows and grafting trees, about not putting potatoes into the same plot in succeeding seasons, about spraying apple trees. But there was too much of it so that, by the time I was seventeen, I felt I had done enough gardening to do me a lifetime.

Today, I am satisfied with a patch of grass with a clipped hedge where I can sit out if the sun shines. I love flowers but am prepared to leave the sowing of seeds, the transplanting and the weeding to others. Yet I ought to have been more grateful for now I realise that all the apples gathered, and raspberries and other fruits plucked, probably helped to pay for my schooling. I know that my parents' dinner often consisted of potatoes and salt, or champ and buttermilk. In view of their sacrifices, I regret that I made so little use of my opportunities at school.

My mother was a woman of many parts. No-one who knew her could ever forget her devotion to my father, or her skill as a wife and mother. She lived a life of self-denial for her husband and children, exercising in her daily life in the home a tolerant, broad-minded, Christian spirit. Few could put on a bandage like her when someone came down from the branch of a tree more quickly than he had gone up. Tongues and hams were pickled. Bread was baked. Scones were made. Marrow, raspberry, rhubarb and other jam was made. While it was my sister's job and mine to wash the dishes after meals, it was seen to be properly done. Our beds and our rooms were our own responsibility: therewas no sweeping of dust under the carpet. Meals were varied and punctual and all was done without any of it being noticed. She was also a skilled seamstress: clothes were made and mended; socks were darned; no lace ever came out of Carrickmacross to excel her crochet work. I remember in particular two large double-bed bed-spreads and several large table-cloths, and many other smaller pieces distinguished by their delicacy.

Another gift of my mother's was that with a hazel-branch she could divine a spring of water. In Malin, all water had to be carried from the neighbouring farm at Priestfield until my mother divined a spring situated under the flagstones at the back door. The Manse was built on solid rock and the men who sank the well had to blast through this, the first trickle of water coming at fourteen feet. It was a definite worry to my parents at this time who or what I might become because of the strong language of the workmen. She also divined the well at the hospital on the Ballygawley Road, Aughnacloy.

Some years ago, I wrote about this, at the request of the editor, in the *Presbyterian Herald*. The result was a spate of letters about the witch at Endor and the "slave girl who hath a spirit of divination". You would have thought my mother practised sorcery did you not realise the fuss was simply another typically Northern Irish religious *non sequitur*. The letters certainly came from people who, whatever their religious stance, never in their lives had to carry a bucket of water for over half-a-mile.

My mother was as firm a believer in total abstinence as my father. One of the pastoral problems in Aughnacloy was that many were introduced to drink on fair days. If a cow was bought or sold the bargain was struck in a pub. When spoken to on the subject, the farmers maintained that if they did not go into the pub they would not be paid and, anyhow, there was nowhere else to go. The result was that my mother organised the women of the congregation and opened a cafe in the McIlwaine Memorial Hall on fair days. The venture was a success and, eventually, many of all denominations clinched their deals there.

One image in particular stands out in my memory. It was that of my mother standing on the steps of the Hall. There was no bread. The IRA had seized it off the train and burned it. To me, as a youngster, who was taught that bread was so valuable that you did not cut off the crusts on sandwiches and that all heels had to be eaten, it was a mystery how anyone could burn bread. Now, of course, I know it was a despicable act at the instigation of some religious, political and educational leaders at a time when many in Ireland were starving. At the same time, I hope that one man was not involved. Charlie was said to be 'the biggest Fenian in the town' and had, on two occasions, enjoyed His Majesty's hospitality on the prison ship Argenta in Belfast Lough. And yet I hope he had no part in the action because Charlie was the first man to give me a drink of tea out of a pint tin in a hayfield. That evening, I felt I was a man. I reject the IRA without equivocation to this day and I hope against hope that Charlie had no hand in making my mother weep.

Like any good presbyterian, my mother could not endure hypocrisy. One of the outstanding illustrations of this occurred when she was shopping in McCullough's Golden Teapot in Waterloo Place, Derry, a few days after Christmas. My father, throughout his ministry, held a service of public worship on Christmas Day. As usual, he had held one in Claremont. In Derry, at that time, there was a rather pugnacious covenanting minister. Spotting my mother, he walked up to her and, in a loud voice for all to hear, declared:

"I see your husband had one of those papist services on Christmas Day".

"Well," my mother replied, "I expect you had turkey and plum pudding".

"Certainly."

"Then," said my mother, "you kept the pagan part of the festival".

My home was one where one lived with God. Naturally, therefore, from an early age I was taught to read and reverence the Bible and to say my prayers. Grace was always said at meal-times. Daily bread is a gift from God. We also had family prayers. The drill was that first a chapter of Scripture was read, followed by prayer. It followed the format of the times before a detailed study of scriptural exposition or child psychology had been undertaken. My father read verse one, my mother the second, myself the third, my sister the fourth. This of course is a completely wrong way to read the Bible because it breaks up the passage and makes it difficult to understand as a unity. This was partly to blame for the fact that, when I was about ten, I declared my hatred of God's action after we had read Genesis XXII. I had placed little Isaac at the centre of the story, not the person the story is really about — Abraham. He lived among people who practised child sacrifice. The problem was Abraham's. Was child sacrifice demanded by Jehovah? It was Abraham who was learning that Jehovah rejected child sacrifice. It was Abraham who was receiving a new and fuller concept of God. My reaction caused quite a stir. I was told how good God was, that Isaac was safe. But no-one told me that Abraham had learned anything: this I had to discover for myself years afterwards. In fact, I hold that the story is not suitable for children under P.9 and perhaps even older. It is a good story but it should be read as a unity after setting out in a few words what it teaches, for example, that it tells us how God taught Abraham about the sacredness of life and that child sacrifice is wrong.

One other incident from family prayers sticks in my mind because of the embarrassing but amusing predicament in which it eventually placed me. I do not remember the exact passage of Scripture, but when it came to my sister's turn to read, the verse contained the name Zerubbabel, which she pronounced 'Sarah Bubble'. She was only eight or or nine. She was corrected, of course, and taught to pronounce the name properly but the event had its repercussions. She was for years nicknamed 'Sarah Bubble' and it became so familiar that I later feared to read a passage containing the name in a church service. I resisted in Drumreagh and in Ballybay and Rockcorry.

However, when in Cooke Centenary, there came a day when a chapter containing the dreaded name had to be used. I read the passage aloud in the study each morning from Monday to Saturday with complete success and, in Cooke on Sunday morning, read 'Sarah Bubble'.

I was taught to say my prayers. Here again, I must make a distinction. I was not really taught to pray — but to "say my prayers". Praying is a much deeper and more difficult process which can only be learned from experience as only very general guidance can be given. Each home, each parent and each child is different.

The practice of grace before meals, family prayer and "saying my prayers" was in a sense a discipline which was a good one but which could have been much more enriching had there been a greater awareness of child-psychology and of children's religious and spiritual development. My parents were not to blame for this, as research in such studies had not then been undertaken. Nevertheless, the discipline was good for me.

In Aughnacloy on Communion Sunday, the Communion Table was covered in a white linen cloth and the paten and chalice were placed on it. Every pew, the Table in the aisle having been given up, was covered with a white linen runner or cloth giving the appearance of a Table. Here, those who were going to communicate took their seats. The children sat in the transept, from which vantage-point they saw their fathers and mothers, the postman, the breadman, the teacher, the doctor and others participate. In a mystical way, they looked forward to the day when they too would sit at the Table of the Lord. This had a profound influence on myself and on others. The action, as always, spoke more clearly than any catechising or sermon.

One Sunday at Loanends, for a reason I cannot recall, I began to think. It may have been something my father had said in the sermon, or something I had read, or my mother had said, or it may have been the anxiety of forthcoming exams. Whatever the cause, I began to think about the purpose of life, what I was going to be, why I was going to university, what kind of job I should look for. As I puzzled upon such things, it suddenly dawned on me that there never had been a time when I was not a Christian. I had been born within His covenant and was a member of His people from birth: "I have always been a Christian". I had to face the significance of that. God demanded a response. I had become aware that God had chosen me through the Christian influence of my home and my father's preaching and example. I had many thoughts, most of them the immature fantasies of a teenager. But one thing was certain: I must become a student for the Christian ministry within the Presbyterian Church which is my spiritual home.

These were some of the relationships and events which helped to make me what I am. Of course, I learned much more: that life is fluid, that one must keep on growing and expanding and be prepared to alter and change, that the past must not be allowed to be a fetter but a starting-point for the future, and, above all, that hope is vital.

2 By Derry's walls

My father was called to be minister of Loanends congregation in the Templepatrick Presbytery in 1926 and was installed on 26 October. This was a time of great change for me. Instead of being a boarder at Campbell College, I became a dayboy at Shaftesbury House. Here I had new vistas, especially in English literature and history, opened up to me. Home was very different too. Aughnacloy Manse had been secluded in pleasant countryside. No one overlooked you except McGirr's and then only if you were over half-way down the avenue. Loanends Manse, on the other hand, sat in a triangle of roads that had come far from being 'loanens'. You were only in private when in the house with the blinds drawn. Aughnacloy had been a mixed community, whereas in Loanends, if one stood at the Manse door and surveyed an area of some four miles, north, south, east, and west, there was nothing but presbyterians.

Most of them were farmers who went to market in Belfast. Leaving home about 6.30 a.m. in the horse and cart, they would sell their buttermilk and farm produce, then start for home. At Ligoniel, they would lie down in the cart and sleep, the well-trained horse stopping at each pub as it came to it, and the barman would come out and waken them so that they might have 'some refreshment'. As for me, I left daily — Saturdays excepted — on the bus about 8.15 and did not return until about 4.30. The chief interest on the journey would often turn out to be courtin' the girls. To be really enjoyed, of course, courtin' involves technique, skill and flair. Even here for a minister's son there was a problem should a father object to "Killinchy mufflers" being given to the same girl regularly. I think my father understood the problem well.

During the winter, I spent my free time playing rugby for Antrim, cycling both ways. In the summer, I rode the bicycle to Dundrod, Crumlin, Aldergrove, Templepatrick, Killead and elsewhere for the motor-racing. In August it came to me, for Loanends was in Grand Prix country, and the Manse was half-way along the seven-mile straight, so I had the thrill of watching Alec Bennett, Tommy Spann and the others displaying their skills. The Ulster Grand Prix was the festival of the year. My eyes danced in my head the first time I saw it, and I am sure that no-one who witnessed it could ever forget the scrap between Graham Walker (Rudge) and Charlie Dodson (Sunbeam) in 1928 or the roaring massed start of that year.

I had to have a motorbike. My father had had a Royal Enfield in Aughnacloy on which I had learned to ride. At Loanends, I got a machine of my own — a Velocette. It did not last long. Complaints about hens being run over, and a tragic accident in which two riders (both members of the congregation) were killed, saw to that. Looking back, it was possibly just as well, though I felt it hard at the time.

My love of motor-bikes remained for years, but gradually faded when the Scotts, Nortons, Sunbeams and AJS's disappeared. The abolition of the old course killed it. No longer did George Brockerton leap for about twenty yards when he hit the hump at the corner. I have been back occasionally, but the glamour has gone.

My father's installation coincided with an extremely important event, the memory of which survives with me to this day, and that was when James "Pope" Hunter of Knock, and his friends, accused Professor J.E. Davey of heresy. They had tried the same on James Haire, but *The Hunter and the Haire,* twenty-seven verses of satire by "Catch-my-pal" Patterson:

> Now list, O Church, "Keep on your Haire!
> Don't let your Haire stand on an end."
> Your best friends to a Haire are knit,
> In bands of steel that nought can bend.
> Let your Professor in his Chair,
> Sit tight and not e'en turn a Haire.

had ridiculed them out of court. Now they went for Davey. Not only was he charged but he was pilloried throughout the country in a public campaign of vilification even when the subject was *sub judice*. The representative elder from Loanends received some of the pamphlets circulating against Professor Davey and came to my father asking him how he should vote. My father told him he should decide how he should vote only on the basis of the debate in the General Assembly and did not state an opinion. The elder was a man of great integrity, thanked my father and followed his advice. One can only wish today that all ministers were honourable enough to adhere to the Reformed doctrine that an elder in higher Courts is a 'representative', not a 'delegate' and that there should be no indoctrination.

The trial itself did not interest me at the time though I have given much thought to it since. What interested me then were the character and tactics of the accusers and the accused, the approach of ministers visiting the Manse, the distortions and lack of integrity on the part of some. I remember one wet day when I had nothing better to do taking one of the booklets which set out the attack on Professor Davey's *The Changing Vesture of the Faith* and checking its quotations from Professor Davey's book. I found over sixty misquotations. Accuracy and truthfulness did not appear to me to have been essential.

The Loanends period of my life was one of physical and mental growth, an opening of mind, a grasping of values, and a realisation of the need for integrity and loyalty, and, of course, it was here that I decided to become a student for the Ministry of the Presbyterian Church in Ireland.

After nearly three years in Loanends, my father was installed in Claremont Presbyterian Church, Derry. As the move to Loanends made him decide that he had no need to pay for me as a boarder at Campbell College when I could live at home, so the move to Derry led him to decide that he did not need to pay for digs for me in Belfast to attend Queen's University when I could live at home and attend Magee College (MCD).

This did not disturb me unduly, until I discovered that, in order the enter MCD, I had to matriculate in Greek, or take it as an additional class over and above the normal work of the first year. I did not know what 'alpha' and 'omega' were, but I hated the prospect of an additional class. So, I took the plunge. On the 29th February, I went to Hemptons and ordered a Greek Grammar, Demosthenes' *Philippics II* and two books of Xenephon's *Anabasis*. Like my father and Uncle John, I worked hard, had a good memory and was able to matriculate and enrol in the autumn.

Derry contained several shocks for me as a teenager. I had never lived anywhere before where I was warned about going into certain areas. I was not forbidden, but I received instructions to take care. Thankfully, I never found myself in any difficulty. I walked the Walls. I read Mackenzie's *Siege of Derry* and saw Walker's account for what it was. More importantly, from the first I knew the Siege to be an European battle between the Hapsburgs and the French fought on Irish soil. I saw in Derry there were two communities living in opposition to each other not because of what were doubtful interpretations of historic fact, but because of the continuation of a seventeenth century attitude of mind. This was carried even into Church relationships. If one went into First Derry Presbyterian Church, St. Columba's Cathedral, or St. Eugene's Cathedral, one could sense it. It appeared in two forms — the Protestant/Roman Catholic and Presbyterian/Anglican. Sadly, Orangeism and Nationalism both used their religion as a political weapon. I do not say their Christianity. The religion of each was a caricature.

I liked Derry and the surrounding hills, its handiness to Fahan and Inch, Grienan and Burt. I liked its quays and the fact one might often be treated to coffee by the crews of trawlers and shown over the ships. I could hear of other lands — Spain, France and Greece. I liked the river and on a Saturday would go walking with friends along the bank of the Foyle to Culmore, take out a boat, and in the evening wander home. Or perhaps it would not be the Foyle, but the Faughan, where, entering at Glendermott, we would wade up the river bed looking for somewhere to fish. The environs of Derry were more attractive than the city itself.

Derry had an excellent Philharmonic Society and perhaps for me its highlight was the year they sang Handel's *Messiah* with Elsie Suddaby as one of the soloists. Sometimes, still, when listening to the work on records, I close my eyes and I can still see her standing there — I'll not say dressed, but rather robed — in spotless white.

Her singing of 'I Know That My Redeemer Liveth' filled me with apocalyptic fascination. Here too, I studied the organ with Morgan Cartright, and music theory with Marie Longwell. Playing duets with Marie was great fun, especially when she finished and I had several notes left over.

At home, my father's illness meant that I had to take a greater responsibility for affairs about the house. As I have said it determined my method of study. I had to win a scholarship or I was out. So I worked for the scholarship examinations and only sought to get the pass mark in the class exams, that is, I worked during the holidays and enjoyed the sporting activities during term. It is not a pattern to be copied, but the fact that my father might die at any minute of the day led me into it if my studies were to continue. Even then there were problems.

Claremont was in many ways a typical presbyterian congregation. Most of them were loyal to my father and supported my mother. They were good attenders and proud of their congregation. But, as is normal, there were some who only attended on Communion Sunday, some who would not attend the Bible Class, and a couple whom even Gabriel could not please.

The greatest influence, however, was MCD which I entered in September 1929. As a student for the Ministry, I was received by the Presbytery of Derry on 20 May 1930, in the Session room in Fahan Church. The events of that evening were to make a deep impression on me. A student, considerably my senior, had to deliver a sermon before the Presbytery. This he did with his hands in his trouser-pockets. When he had finished, before the content was discussed, "his insulting manner" in addressing the Presbytery with his hands in his pockets was considered on the proposal of the Rev. William Ross of Burt. His manners were not those of a gentleman. He might even behave in this way in the pulpit. The members of Presbytery clearly held that they had a responsibility in this regard. Sadly, there are those today who appear to be ashamed of the Genevan preacher's gown. While not being a great one for dressing up, from that evening I have believed that there is a great deal to be said for treating one's congregation or a Court of the Church with respect.

In my time MCD was a small College consisting of seven professors and five lecturers, with approximately 130-140 students.

It was friendly and homely. Each professor knew every student personally. All the students knew each other. In many ways it resembled a family. Everyone was interested in the welfare of his fellows. It also had a distinguished academic record. Each year the majority of the *respondentes* in the Bachelor of Arts degree examinations were Mageemen and women. Each year, they also provided a fairish quota of honours graduates. In many ways the Academic staff resembled personal tutors. While one might have a closer relationship with some fellow students than others it would be unfair to think of anyone not being an acquaintance or a friend. Most of the male students were students for the Ministry of the Presbyterian Church, but there always was a number preparing to be teachers, medical doctors, or candidates for the legal profession. They were drawn from various backgrounds — farms, manses, Saorstat Éireann, teachers, missionaries. The MCD motto probably fitted us, *Fac et Spera* (Do and Hope). Of course some of us excelled in *Spera,* because there had not been enough *Fac.*

We had a debating society on Fridays, table-tennis, tennis in summer, rugby, hockey, and several soccer teams. Many a good game was played on the "hump", now a car park. Practically every student played games, and many excelled in several. It was quite a thrill to play with the battle-cry: "Magee is up the river" ringing in one's ears. The charm, friendships, disappointments and laughter of those days did much to make me. There was Bill Haslett, Moreland Kennedy, Peter Wightman, Jimmie Kilgore, Bill M'Comb, Hazie Hunter, Stuart Black, Rex Rutherford, Bowie Thompson, Hoots Gibson, Jap Langtry, Ernie Stronge, Sammy Watt, Charlie Huggins, to name a just a few.

Of course there were many pranks and one had, not infrequently, to be on the lookout. One of the most amusing was the day Mr Thomas Finnegan in the Latin class called on J.A.P. (Jap) Langtry to translate. J.J. (Hoots) Gibson was sitting on his right. Hoots was a good Latin scholar, and Jap was not. Except that it was out of Livy, I have forgotten the passage. Jap's immediate reaction was to say, "Help me, boys". This Gibson proved all too ready to do. So it started, Gibson saying a phrase with Jap repeating it. It ran something like this:

The inhabitants put up a strong resistance so the Roman general laid siege to the city. For some days attack followed attack but met with strong counter-attacks. So the general decided to make one all-out effort. It was successful and, greatly rejoicing as evening came, the soldiers enjoyed themselves by taking the dusky Carthaginian maidens to the sandhills.

With the word "sandhills" producing memories of episodes when camping out at Portrush, there was an uproar as Jap realised that he had not been translating but repeating a figment of Gibson's imagination. To be fair, all Finnegan said was, "Quite an interesting translation, Mr. Gibson".

Professor James McMaster lectured me in Greek in my first year. It was his final class. He made a deep impression on me because, though blind, he sat there quoting the text in Greek and expounding it with a vision that those of us who had our sight did not possess. Having just matriculated, I knew little about Classical and Doric and such things but I was filled with enthusiasm for Greek culture and mythology, and was inspired to continue classical Greek for a further two years.

Professor R.J. Semple taught English and History. White-haired and distinguished-looking he presided over his classes with a benevolent calm. He was a real Shakespearean character. The professor who influenced me most, however, was Mr George B. Woodburn, who lectured in Logic, Empiricism and the philosophy of Kant.

I remember little about the first year except that we were informed that, in TCD, three marks were deducted for every spelling mistake in essays and if there were three it was torn up. I do not know if this was true as I never risked it. Fortunately, Aughnacloy had taught me how to spell as well as count.

During the second year I was beginning what might be called my 'communist' period. I read Marx and Engels, Laski, Sydney and Beatrice Webb, Orwell and James Maxton. *Animal Farm* even approached the heights of *Gulliver's Travels,* which I knew to be a parabolic account of Ireland's struggle for freedom. Into this arena was flung the request to write an essay on The House of Lords. With true literary flair and demagogic reasoning and irony, I dealt a death blow to the Lords. The essays were returned in class one by one until only one was left — mine. The old man said rather sadly, "If my hair was not grey already this essay would turn it grey that anyone could say such things about the House of Lords". He had given it nought. He did not condemn or refute. He was just sad. That hit me hard. I had not intended to hurt him. In fact, when writing about the Lords I had never even thought of him. I was chastened. Since then I have learned much and support a bicameral constitution. At the same time, I reject any method which fills a Senate with people simply because they in their dreams fought at the battle of the Boyne or were in the Post Office. The structure of an Upper House is still unresolved in Ireland for party-politics plays too big a part, which must be eradicated.

Here, though, I should finish with my 'communist' flirtation, which even led me to book a trip to Moscow in the mid-thirties. I never went. But only because the trip was cancelled: not enough people had applied. Hegel had described his philosophy as the New Testament expressed in terms of pure thought. With this, having read W.T. Stace and Edward Caird, I was prepared to agree. Marx and Engels had taken Hegelian philosophy and applied it to the field of economics. Here, however, was a difficulty for while Hegel's thought applied to the whole of life, Marx and Engels limited its relevance. Further, from reading the Webbs the Soviet State did not appear to me to apply Hegelianism sufficiently objectively. It was too narrow. For this reason, namely, that man is spiritual and moral as well as physical, I came to regard the communist system as defective. This, of course, gained me £50 for the Gailey Essay. Communism in theory had many fine humanitarian slogans — wholly in the spirit of Christ — but as the Dutch socialist, Troelstro, says "its basis is too restricted and its methods too one-sided".

All the same, it influenced me. In 1944, in one of my congregations there was a farmer who was poor and his horse died. So the countryside did one of those nice things which country people do. They decided to raise money to buy him a new horse. I was asked to announce this from the pulpit, which I was glad to do. In doing so I said, "What you are doing is generous and something to be proud of, but you know what we really ought to be doing is attempting not only to buy him a horse but to set him up so that, if this horse should die, he would be able to retain his dignity and buy one for himself".

Shock-waves throughout the district!

"The minister is a communist!".

"The minister is a socialist!".

While charity is necessary, at times there is something beyond charity and that is human rights. Calvin saw this when he discussed the stewardship of money, as Bieler makes clear in *The Social Humanism of Calvin*. I still believe that I, while upholding charity, was standing for a Gospel principle.

MCD, its staff and students, its surroundings and attitude to life, its history and ideals, contributed much to the making of me. I generally enjoy what I am doing. When working, I worked hard with no thought of play, and when I played I did so with no thought of work. Enjoying what I was doing, as I did it, has been a feature of my life and it was Magee which taught me this.

Magee students had to attend lectures in Trinity College, Dublin, in the Hilary and Trinity terms in the third year and Trinity in the fourth before sitting the honours degree examination. Our first experience of Dublin came when we had to go to TCD for the Final Freshman Examination, commonly known as "Little-Go". Having all dutifully thrown our penny into the Boyne as the train crossed the bridge at Drogheda our hope was that luck was with us. The arrival at Amiens Street station, now Connolly, was not too enticing for we were almost swallowed by a crowd of begging children. Thankfully, this is no longer true. This was a two-day visit with most of the time spent in the Examination Hall answering papers or the much-feared vivas, so we saw little of the city. However, after spending Trinity term in the following year and visiting the sights, I came to like Dublin, even if the guide at Kilmainham Gaol did not know which was Sinclair Kelburn's cell. As for Trinity College itself it provided a broadening of outlook, a relaxing of attitude, a wider perspective and that can only have been beneficial.

One of the events I will never forget was hearing Eamonn de Valéra's election speech in College Green. He was not an orator like Dillon, but won support for his cause by the substance of what he said. In a way, the gathering was not simply a political meeting, but an assembly of devotees. While not accepting his political outlook, it is only fair to say that I found him honourable according to his principles in the various dealings I was to have with him on behalf of my Church and congregation.

In Trinity, Dr. A.A. Luce lectured me on Malebranche and Berkeley. One had always to be very careful when he asked a question, "Barkley, what is in this bottle?" If I answered "ink" he replied, "No, Barkley. It is glass". Of course, if I had said "glass" he would have said "ink". If I happened to be looking out the window to see what was happening at Westland Row station, this was cut short by "What does Barkley in the flesh think?" Not infrequently, Barkley in the flesh was weighed in the balance and found wanting. His lectures on Malebranche were stimulating and his interpretation of his philosophy individual. His great virtue, however, was that he made one think. There were no easy answers. The opinion of another was never to be taken as a solution. One had to find this for himself. My father had taught me to think for myself and be independent. Dr. Luce stimulated this outlook, advanced it, and laid the basis for this approach to be adopted in New Testament exegesis and theology later in Professor Davey's classes.

My other lecturer was Mr. H.S. Macran, who lectured on Hegel. There were many rumours about him. He was "the only man who really understood the philosophy of Hegel except Hegel himself". Another was that at times "he got very drunk". This led us to pester him in class with the question, "Should a lecturer in moral philosophy himself be moral?" For all I know he may never have partaken of anything stronger than tea, but the rumour (true or false) determined our behaviour. Mr. Macran was easily the most brilliant lecturer I ever had. In he came to class, sat down, reached for his pencil in the right hand pocket, it wasn't there, he reached to the left, took it out, rolled it between the thumb and first two fingers of his two hands, and lectured without a book or a note. It was like a stream of fresh water bubbling from a spring. Every day the routine was the same. Brilliant exposition, brilliant cross-references to other philosophers, brilliant detail and summary, brilliant and thrilling. Thesis, antithesis, synthesis — they formed a mighty river of thought in his philosophy of history and of religion. This equipped me for studying Edward Caird's *Evolution of Theology in the Greek Philosophers* and William Temple's Gifford Lectures with great enthusiasm at a later date.

His teaching also had a more immediate and drastic influence. I had done fairly well in the Senior Freshman and Junior Sophister examinations in philosophy, so loving the subject I decided to work hard and do well in the degree.

It ended in disaster. I did work hard. Whether it was overwork or nerves I do not know but, during the week of the degree examinations, I dreamed the stuff at night (generally mixing it up in every possible way), woke regularly unable to solve a mental or moral question, could not remember facts or reasons when attempting to answer the papers, and ended up with a third class honours degree. To me, this was a disaster. I was back again in the old predicament of doing just enough in class to pass and hoping to get a scholarship in September. The flimsy short-lived desire to excel had gone.

After my first year at Magee College, I hoped to go to New College, Edinburgh, because my father had been there but I was refused permission to go unless I was prepared to take an extra year in Hebrew, because the courses in Hebrew were not similar. Financially, this was an utter impossibility. The result was that my final two years were taken at The Presbyterian College (or Assembly's College, now Union Theological College), Belfast.

One of the features of life in Assembly's College was the rivalry between Queensmen and Mageemen. It was always friendly but could be serious. We had a very distinguished elocution teacher, but the Mageemen thought he had favourites. Dissatisfaction came to a head when he entered five Queensmen for the public speaking contest at the Belfast Feis. Our dignity was offended. Something had to be done. So each of us subscribed sixpence and we entered Moreland Kennedy — who had drawn the short straw — for the competition. The great night arrived, the candidates came and went, and Morely got a great reception. The ajudication followed: "I award first place to R.S.M..." there was uproar. I don't think anyone heard the word Kennedy, and if the ajudicator had anything more to say it was never said. Proceedings halted as Morely was carried shoulder high up one aisle and down the other, while the rafters rang with "Magee is up the river". It was a never to be forgotten night. Sadly Ireland appreciated neither the man nor his gifts, and our pal died in exile in Canada, but he sure did Magee proud that night.

In those days there were no students' grants. The Students' Bursary Fund promised to give any one £5, if he could prove he needed it. Every penny had to be watched and sometimes we were literally penniless. In the latter circumstances we had to arrange our own amusement. Often it consisted in going down to Garfield Street or Arthur Square or the Customs House steps and taking on one of the various speakers in debate. The subject did not matter. It might be the Christadelphian doctrine that women could not receive the Holy Spirit, the necessity for socialism, Stormont misrule, the need for the Labour Party, or Irish nationalism. This was very good for us and we learned a lot. It taught us to think on our feet. It taught us to give one's opponent a fair hearing and how to be gracious in adversity. Immediately, there was any unfair play or accusation you lost the support of the crowd. One had always to be prepared for getting caught in cross-fire.

One of my great pleasures was being taught by the church's alleged heretic, Professor J.E. Davey. Davey had had a grim time. After a hearing lasting for fourteen sessions the Presbytery of Belfast had acquitted him, and the accusers appealed to the General Assembly. The appeal was dismissed. To quote a non-Irish independent opinion, the *British Weekly,* the following week, reported:

as the Trial progressed, it became amazingly clear that Professor Davey stood quite unexpectedly close to the subordinate standards. He seemed indeed to be the most loyal Calvinist of us all. The accusers, on the other hand, again and again involved themselves in the meshes of outworn heresies, returning with pathetic insistence to the Docetist. A counter charge, had it been worthwhile, would have been a simple matter.

The verdict had been arrived at in a constitutional and democratic manner and was accepted by the church, but there were others who continued the campaign of distortion, misrepresentation, and vilification. One such instance was a turning point in my life. The incident occurred on Sunday, 19 November, 1933, a full six years after the acquittal.

The Presbyterian Church had a number of great orators at that time and, as there were no assistantships, the students were insatiable sermon tasters. So four of us went that evening to hear one of them. When he saw us in the gallery, he forgot his calling and gave, not a sermon, but a tirade — interspersed every few sentences with "and you four boys on the gallery can go back to Assembly's College and tell them that". When he ran out of abusive language he said, "Let us

now sing what is the will of God for Professor Davey and all like
him, Psalm 109, verses 8-13":

> Few be his days, and in his room
> His charge another take.
> His children let be fatherless,
> His wife a widow make.

Some shouted "Hallelujah!" I can still feel the chill that ran down
my spine, and the vivid feeling that the Holy Spirit had forsaken us.

So far as I remember, none of us spoke as we walked back to
College. Had I not been nurtured in the Faith in home and church I
might have mistaken what I experienced that evening as Christianity
instead of seeing it for what it was — pure, pagan hatred
masquerading as the Gospel. Though the greatest scholar Irish
presbyterianism has produced, Professor Davey had to withstand
such vilification all his life. And yet he was one of the most Christian
men I knew. No-one ever heard him speak a harsh or critical word
about those who attacked him in this way. He stood for objective
study and thinking for one's self. I remember him discussing a
problem when a student asked:

"Sir, if you were preaching would you preach that?"

"Certainly".

"Sir, if you were teaching a Sunday School class, would you teach
that?"

"Certainly".

"Sir, is that not a very dangerous thing to teach?"

"Do you mean to tell me Mr — that you are a fifth year student
for the Ministry of the Christian Church and you haven't yet learned
that the New Testament is a dangerous book?"

The use of the term dangerous book helped me to see the New
Testament not so much as a text to be studied as a potent force for
good in the world. This was revolutionary. He helped us to see that
Christianity must be able to stand in its own right in face of criticisms
the same as any other subject. So we should face all questions with a
critical openness. Above all, he taught us that Christianity is not a
system of rules, but a spirit in which one must live.

Principal F.J. Paul lectured in Church History and Symbolics. The
great thing about Principal Paul was that all his work was done with

such meticulous care that one can quote him with the certainty that no one is going to be able to challenge the accuracy of it. His *Romanism and Evangelical Christianity*, though now out of date, being pre-Vatican II, is still valuable as a mine of historical information and an excellent example of the historical method of treating dogma. In showing me that nothing is gained by misrepresentation, and that indulging in it means that your cause is morally lost, he influenced me greatly.

Principal Paul's lectures were very factual, and based upon the writings of the Fathers and Reformers. His knowledge of Patristics in particular was extensive. However, to me his emphasis appeared to be on events, not people; on decrees, not life; on structures, not spirit. His writings and lectures are significant for their erudition and influence. All of us must have been enriched and our knowledge greatly increased from his classes. At the same time I regarded the whole scheme for Church history as defective. Did God not exist before the apostolic age? Did God die in 461? Where was God between 461 and 1325? Did God come alive again in 1325 and die in 1415? Did he die from 1415 until 1483? Did God finally die in 1647 with the adoption of the Westminster *Confession of Faith* by the General Assembly of the Church of Scotland? Of course, I knew God was alive, but I was sufficient of a radical and activist to wonder why nothing sufficiently important to deserve mention happened during the big gaps.

The sixth year history text, J.B. Woodburn's *Ulster Scot* was also something of a revelation. I had been taught Irish history at school, but always in a European or British context. There was nothing wrong with this, but it meant that the *Ulster Scot* was the first detailed study in Irish history *per se* that I had read. Not that I would advocate the narrowly local. Perspective is vital. For example, the Glorious Revolution was not primarily the placing of a Protestant king, instead of a Roman Catholic, on the English throne, but the removal of a despot and the establishment of parliamentary rule; and the Boyne decided whether Louis XIV of France or the Papacy and Hapsburgs would govern Europe.

At the twelfth of July celebrations in 1988 it was claimed, "What we want to establish is the freedom we enjoyed from 1690 to 1972". But who is this "we"? It surely cannot include presbyterians, who suffered under the Sacramental Test Act, under which the Sovereign David Buttle, son of the presbyterian minister of Ballymena, and eight burgesses were turned out of office in Belfast, as were twelve aldermen and fourteen burgesses in Derry. Under it presbyterians could hold no public office under the crown and the validity of their marriages was denied. Is this the 'freedom' the Orange leaders really seek? What I am as a presbyterian and a blackmouth rebels against such a concept of freedom for my country. That is not 'liberty'. It is barely toleration.

Another factor was that we did not do our practical training in readymade Bible classes, or youth clubs, or GGs or BBs. In my final year, I was appointed to work in a YMCA Club in Linenhall Street. Tom Blakely (China and Cork) had been its leader, and several of us were asked to assist his successor, Andy Anderson (Newcastle). So far as I remember, all the members with one exception were unemployed. He had a milk round. We were to take a Bible Class, on Wednesday evenings. The attendance was about eight to twelve. It remained like this for several weeks, so as we had had quite a useful soccer team in Magee with Andy's permission we challenged them to a football match. It was played at Musgrave Park and ended in a three all draw. We were quite pleased as we were a bit out of training and they had several Barn, Queen's Island, and Distillery players. Within a fortnight numbers at the Bible Class had increased to about forty and they challenged us to a return match. This was played in the Ormeau Park and we won one nil.

Only someone who worked in Belfast in 1934-35 can even guess at the poverty and deprivation. An excellent introduction is Robert Harbinson's novel *No Surrender,* which should be followed up by reading his *Song of Erne, Up Spake the Cabin Boy,* and *The Protégé.* At the request of the members of the Club, we organised a league of ten teams for unemployed clubs with a couple of games several days each week in the Ormeau Park; and poor as we were we bought a set of medals for the winners. Andy did not play himself but he was always on the touchline to give his support. All this had certain results. The members asked us also to hold a Service on Sunday evenings to which they could bring their girls. I learned again here that office means little, what is essential is to try to be a person.

In those days there were few assistantships and no assignments.

You had to preach on trial to get an assistantship. Eight of us preached for the assistantship of Richview when I was appointed though I think several had withdrawn before a decision was taken. I know that I was not the first choice. Some of my contemporaries never became assistants or got congregations and went into law, teaching, or farming, others had to go overseas principally to Canada and Scotland.

Richview congregation was a union in 1920 of Donegall Road and Fountainville, which had been burned down in the troubles. Most of the Session were 'fundamentalist' and reactionary in outlook, and the membership numbered about one thousand families with most of them unemployed. My salary was £80 a year, increased to £100 after I was licensed by the Presbytery of Derry on 19 May, 1935. Digs were 35/- a week. No wonder I stood up with only £5.14/- in my pocket to keep me for the next three months on the day of my ordination.

It was hard work. New houses were being built above Broadway at the bog meadows. They had to be visited. Many evenings there were riots. That meant a turn on police Crossley tenders appealing for calm and to the people to go home. What was home? Sometimes it was thirteen or fourteen living in one room with two palliasses of straw for beds and an upturned tea chest for a table. While many were more comfortable, such conditions were widespread. Destitution was everywhere. When going out on pastoral visits you only took tuppence in your pocket for the tram to take you where you were going and bring you back. You dare not have money in your possession or give it. All relief had to be done by docket to a grocer who could be trusted not to give money in exchange.

Solving some of these problems was not easy. I remember on one occasion, at the end of June, a Mrs A. of 31 Clementine Street calling at the digs and my giving her a relief food docket.

In August, when I returned to my digs on the evening of the 10th, my landlady said, "Mrs B. of 31 Clementine Street, called. There is no food in the house".

I did not remember the name but I remembered the number and the street. This made me suspicious so I checked my records to find that in addition to Mrs A, a Mrs C, 31 Clementine Street, had got a docket in April. As the message said "no food in the house", I rose

early the next morning and was at 31 Clementine Street shortly after
8.30 with bread, butter, bacon, eggs, milk and tea. On the door being
opened the following conversation took place:

"Good morning, Mrs A. Is Mrs B. in?"

"I'm Mrs B."

"Oh no, you're not. You're Mrs A."

"No! I'm Mrs B."

"Tell me, is Mrs C in?"

Apparently this took her by surprise and she replied

"I'm Mrs C."

"How can you be Mrs C. and also Mrs B. and also
Mrs A.?"

"Because we are starving".

The sooner those people who complain about the poor today read
Harbinson's four novels the better. There they will get a true picture
of the bravery and distress of the destitute.

After six months in Richview during the summer of 1935, I was
called to Drumreagh Presbyterian Church, Ballymoney, and was
ordained there by the Presbytery of Route on 24 September, 1935.

3 The Meetinghouse at the Cross

In my final weekend in College, I received my one and only supply from the Pulpit-Supply secretary. It was to go to Drumreagh, a vacant congregation, as supply the following day. I had never heard of the place. I took the train to Ballymoney and was met by a stern-looking old man, the Rev. Samuel Wallace, who took me out to the Meetinghouse. During the service I had to repeat an announcement, which had been made by the convener of the vacancy the previous week, that the candidates for the vacancy would start preaching on trial the following Sabbath, which I read as Sunday. Every Sunday Mr. Wallace took Louis Blair's taxi out to Church and gave a lift to an old lady in her sixties called Mrs. M'Dowell. On the way back to Ballymoney, Mr. Wallace asked her what she thought of me:

"Oh, he's a nice young man if he wouldn't call the Sabbath Sunday".

So far as I was concerned that was that.

Six weeks later I received a phone call from the Rev. H.C. Waddell, convener of the vacancy, asking me if I would accept a Call to Drumreagh. I replied in the negative, pointing out that I was not eligible for a Call as I had not served an assistantship. They then had a second list. Again the convener wrote offering me a Call, which I again refused. Even so the congregation met and made out to me a unanimous Call, and not only that but brought it down to me that evening in Portstewart, where I was on holiday with my father and

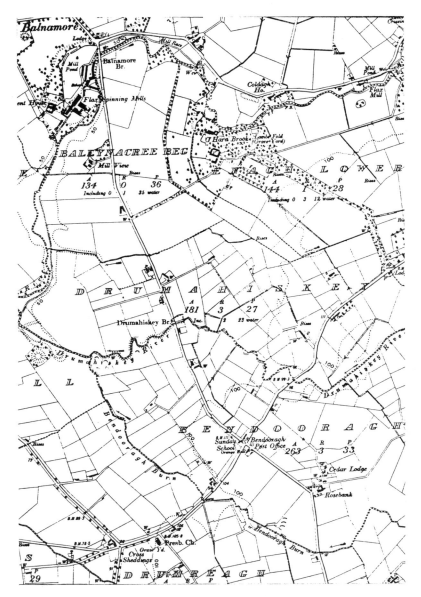

Drumreagh, County Antrim, in the 1930s, showing Balnamore Mill Village to the north, and the Meetinghouse (marked Presb. Ch.) bottom left.

mother, saying they would postpone the ordination until I was eligible. In the light of this, I felt I dare not refuse as there must be some reason for it.

My father and mother came down for the service of Ordination, but that morning my father had one of his serious turns and was unable to attend. Fortunately, as the day advanced, he recovered sufficiently to be able to attend the reception for a short time.

The Service was solemn and dignified. I answered the prescribed questions, signed the Confession of Faith, and the Rev. H.C. Waddell (Trinity), convener of the vacancy, gave the Charge. It was a very amiable occasion, five of the ministers present having been fellow-students and others being friends of the family.

Then came the reception in the High Street Café, Ballymoney, the meal being followed by the usual hearty toasts and speeches. The first toast, 'Prosperity to Ireland', was replied to by Mr. W.V. M'Cleery, M.P., later minister of Labour and afterwards of Commerce. This toast, normally responded to by a prominent layman in the local community, remained the custom until about 1937. Following Éire's adoption of a new constitution, some began to use it for party-political purposes, and when Éire became neutral in 1939, the custom fell into desuetude. This to my mind is a tragedy as it has taken away from the Church an opportunity to witness to the fact that her mission is to the whole island. Though the Church claims to be, under God, the Presbyterian Church in Ireland, one is sometimes tempted to ask if this is so in fact, or just in name.

Toasts followed to the General Assembly and the Colleges, responded to by Principal Paul and President G.B. Woodburn respectively. The Rev. Waddell then proposed the toast of the new minister to which I responded by thanking my parents, teachers and fellow-students, and concluding:

The people of Drumreagh congregation have conferred on me a great honour in asking me to become their minister, for which I thank them; and I hope I shall never betray their trust and confidence. To them I admit my unworthiness. However, with Mr. Wallace to keep me right, I have nothing to fear. I perhaps shall make mistakes, but I hope you will forgive me if I do. I ask you help and sustain me by your prayers. Also I hope and trust you will find me always and in all things an ambassador for Christ.

I hope that in some small measure I was able to fulfil this.

Toasts to the Presbyteries of Derry and Belfast followed and were responded to by the Rev. John Brewster (Fahan and Inch) and the Rev. Robert Anderson (Richview) respectively. Mr. J.J. Gibson, a fellow-student at MCD, who was later to have a distinguished career in the legal profession, becoming Probate Registrar for Londonderry, spoke on behalf of the students. Though he only died a few years ago, our paths in life never crossed again since that day, and as I write my hope is that I have been worthy of the character he gave me then as a champion of right, justice, and the less fortunate. The proceedings ended with my father proposing a toast to the Rev. Samuel Wallace, senior minister of the congregation. He responded in the style of dry Ulster humour in which he excelled. In the evening, there was the congregational soirée, with tea and soirée-bread followed by musical items and speeches laced with wit, laughter, and goodwill lasting into the wee small hours. Yes, in those days an Ordination was a great event not only for the ordinand, but for the whole community. It was a day of hope and rejoicing for all.

On the day following my ordination I made a vow to buy a decent book each month (by which was meant one valued about £2-£5 at that time), and if I had not finished it by the end of the month, to buy a learned commentary on a book of the Bible. Unlike most of my new year resolutions, this was never broken until I was appointed a professor in 1954.

Drumreagh lies about two miles out of Ballymoney on the Co. Derry side. It was a farming community, with Balnamore mill village as its northern boundary. The Meetinghouse is at the Cross, before one comes to the Agivey Bridge across the Bann. It is a barn church with a gallery right round, which meant that, when in the pulpit, the Calderwoods and Moores could see me tying my shoelaces. The vestry and session room in my time was at the top of the stairs behind the back gallery. This meant that one had to come down the stairs, and walk up the aisle when going to the pulpit. A more intimidating descent, or rather ascent, to the pulpit has surely never been devised.

The congregation consisted of about ninety-six small farmers, with one large farmer, Thomas Fulton, a 'white man' if ever there was one, who described his life to me as working an acre a day throughout the year and having a day's holiday every leap-year. From this, I regarded him as farming 365 acres. He was precentor in my time as there was no organ. Later he was ordained an elder and became session-clerk, in which office he has been succeeded by his son James, who is very much his father's son.

Most of the farmers were hardworking and relatively poor, for the days of farming prosperity and subsidies had not yet dawned. They certainly lived up to the 'protestant work ethic', probably believing that the concept came from John Calvin when it really comes from Benjamin Franklin. It meant hard work based on thrift and integrity for the common welfare.

This they applied to all aspects of life — including the minister's. The Manse was completely new, and sat in a bit from the road in a field. One evening, about a week after my ordination, I went out to examine the situation with a view to planting a hedge, when along came a member of the congregation. He stopped and greeted me with the remark:

"You're not working th' night, your reverence. You're not visiting". Benjamin Franklin has a lot to answer for!

In Balnamore mill village, there were about thirty families. Living conditions were atrocious. Going from the Manse as one turned into the village there was a row of houses on the left and another on the right and, beyond them, the mill dam. The roadway into the mill was full of pot holes filled with water and slush. It was quite common to see the women and girls in bare feet wearing a flimsy frock (with nothing underneath, so I was told), walking across this on a winter's evening with the sweat of their work still lashing from them. No wonder the place was rife with tuberculosis. The houses in the Red Row and the Grey Row further up were much better. All the village houses had electric light, DC run off the dynamo of the mill, but earthen floors. You can guess what that was like on a winter's night with snow on the ground. There was a pump at the end of the dam, but you dare not use it as the dam water seeped into the well and the dam was the last earthly resting place for old bicycles, used tyres, and dead cats and dogs. This meant that all water had to be carried from beside the Grey Row, some quarter of a mile or so away.

Living conditions were such that I saw something must be done about it so, with the help of Mr W.V. M'Cleery and William

Mulholland, in 1936 a club for the men and boys of the village was started. It was open six nights in the week, except the Church needed the hall. It had only two rules — No Drink and No Gambling. We played various indoor games, for example, darts, dominoes, draughts, and had a football team. The club was open to everyone, Protestant and Roman Catholic alike. Balnamore has many happy memories, not only of the Davidsons and M'Nabbs, but also of the Connors and Scullions. The club made a real contribution to goodwill in the community.

My Balnamore Bible Class included the three Mulhollands, a couple of the Davidsons, Alec M'Nab, Willie M'Kinney (now an elder in the congregation), Tommy Johnston, and James M'Caldridge, and others. Being a Bible Class we studied the Scriptures and all brought a Bible with them. About my third Sunday, I asked James to read a verse. I was so ashamed. I did not know James could neither read nor write. He could sign his name, not by writing it but by drawing it the same way one would draw a cow or a horse. I got a great shaking up that night.

There were three elders in the congregation — William Glass, William James Calderwood, and John Finlay. They were great old men, each very much an individual. William James was the most prominent because he was also congregational treasurer. The proceedings of the Kirk-session were most harmonious. On the other hand, my first meeting of committee hadn't right started until one member sent another to hell. The reply was, "I'll see you there as you're a fool". Then somewhat typically came the claim, "I'm a fool for Christ's sake". I knew *The Code* said I should call on both to apologise, but I wasn't sure they would. Further I knew that if I did so, each would feel humiliated before his peers and so I would be making two enemies for life, which was no way to start a ministry. So I simply said:

Gentlemen, we met this evening to do the work of Christ's Church. God who made eternity also made time so he is in no hurry. We are not in the spirit to do the Church's work tonight. So I adjourn this meeting until this day next week. Stand for the benediction.

One must be absolutely firm, but without any rod of iron. When making my way back to the Manse a man stepped out from the hedge at Caulfield's:

"Mr. Barkley, I am sorry about what happened this evening, but remember you can learn from it".

"Learn what?"

"No one has any defence against ignorance"!

I never forgot that and have often been grateful for William Mulholland's insight. In fairness, I must emphasise that nothing even remotely similar ever occurred again. William Mulholland was congregational secretary, and a kind of father to me, and his sons — Danny, Andy and Billy — were like younger brothers. It was great to chat to Daniel Mulholland, formerly a lecturer in Chemical Engineering in the University of London, about old times at the 150th celebrations of the Meeting House in 1988. I was much touched by his thanks to me for having helped him with his maths when he was a boy. I hadn't remembered a thing about it. He was the last of the family, and my life became much poorer as the result of his death in 1989.

So far as I know my preaching was acceptable, although as far as William James, was concerned:

"It's not worth while now changing your clothes to come to meetin' the service is so short".

When I offered to put it to a vote of the congregation, he laughed:

"Nae! Nae! They're all for ye".

My preaching was mostly expository, as it remained throughout my pastoral ministry. Exposition of the Word is to me basic and essential. However, William James did get the delight of scoring a point on one occasion. It was over a paraphrase. I had preached to the children about ants. So as they did not sing hymns I used paraphrase twelve "View the ant's labours and be wise", continued the Service and closed as usual with a paraphrase and the Apostolic Benediction. William James and I met at the door out of the gallery:

"You're niver to do the like o' that agin".

Somewhat surprised, I enquired, "What did I do?"

"You're niver to do the like o' that agin. Two paraphrases in the one Service; they couldn't both be inspired".

William James taught me much, for while our views on 'inspiration' may have differed we were bound together by a common love of presbyterianism. Within two years, both hymnody and instrumental music were accepted.

Much of one's pastoral ministry must forever remain a closed book. The events are personal and private. The sons and daughters of those involved survive. Their privacy must be respected. I met with many sorrows, problems, fears, suspicions, hatreds and suchlike. They are for no one's ears.

The shadow of the Rev. Samuel Wallace loomed over my pastoral ministry, for after him I was considered a bad visitor. This was because if anyone was sick in Kiddymaddy, or Eden, when Mr. Wallace visited the sick person he also called with every family in the townland, whereas I only visited the home of the sick person. No-one said, so it was some time before I became aware of my failure in this regard, yet I don't think anyone was overlooked or neglected. The sick were visited weekly or oftener if serious, and all houses were visited pastorally three times in two years.

Visiting was always enjoyable and I cannot remember a single really unpleasant incident. Of course, even Mr. Wallace had somewhat departed from the ritualistic, catechetical style of visiting of former days, and this was further extended in my time. My aim was always to establish trust and friendship. There were happy occasions as when I was able to get Hester Stevenson of Drumlee, who had been in bed for some eight or nine years from the day of her husband's funeral, to rise and try to walk. She took too much out of herself the following day and so landed back in bed again, but it was only for a day. Having learned patience she progressed slowly, and eventually when I was visiting she would tell me how she had enjoyed a dance she had been at the previous week, or where she had been able to go.

Literature on Divine healing was meagre then, but I did study in detail the rites for Visitation of the Sick. I also was familiar with country traditions about faith healing and the existence of the Doon Well, near Kilmacrennan. This was a great help to me throughout my ministry especially when seeking to give confidence to those who were ill. Mrs. M'Mullan comes vividly to mind. She lived with her daughter Mary in Charlotte Street. She had become a communicant when she was fifteen some fifty years before and from that day she had never failed to be present at the Sacrament of the Lord's Supper. She took ill in the autumn of 1938. Her sole desire was to be fit enough to attend the October Communion. That was the purpose of her living, but in the providence of God it was not to be. When I visited her on the Monday after Communion she had failed badly, dying later in the week. The final blow for her was in not being able to be present at the Table of the Lord.

Warm memories come to me too. There was the consternation of Miss Cooper when her brother Boyd would, under the table, nip his small niece to make her squeal when I was saying grace. There was James Macdonald's attempts to make me believe that the Session had made him resign being precentor because he had got false teeth and "they were against instrumental music".

Jem, Thomas, Sarah, Elsie, Hugh, Edith and Ruth all attended the Church Sunday School, were members of the League of Church Loyalty, and attended Balnamore Sunday School. That meant they were entitled to three prizes each every year. Their father allowed them only to take Bibles. That meant eighteen Bibles went into the house each year and they were all kept in a bookcase in the sitting room. I succeeded once in getting a change by pleading for Jem, who was learning to play the piano, to have permission to get a music copy of *Redemption Songs*. Jem was later to give her life trying to save her husband from drowning at Portstewart.

There was Helen M'Kinney, aged two years, sitting on her mother's knee, repeating the whole of the 23rd psalm without a prompt. There was Walker's where I conducted my first baptism, baptising James. There was Pollock's, where with his wife and children sitting round the kitchen, I baptised the father who was in his sixties so that he might become a communicant. In Presbyterianism, the Sacrament of Baptism should always, except in a case of emergency, be celebrated "in the face of the congregation" at the hour of public worship on the Lord's Day. Baptisms were always conducted in the home, and try as I might I could not get the practice changed.

Occasionally, one ran into a problem. I always started a day's visitation at the house farthest from the manse and worked homewards. This day, shortly after dark, I arrived at the last house. Pulling up the car I knocked the door to hear the father (who said at times he was a Plymouth brother and at others he was a member, but who sent his children to the Sunday School), say to the eldest wee girl, aged about ten:

"Tell him there's nobody in".

Which she did. So I simply said, "Tell your father I will call back at another time".

I was angry at the teaching of the child to be deceitful, so I got into the car, drove up the road about a quarter of a mile, and walked back, and knocked. The father opened the door. I said, "Good evening" and he invited me in. He had a very uncomfortable evening especially when we discussed such topics as teaching children to be truthful and honest. He knew I had heard him, so it did not need to be mentioned.

It was an interesting community in which something was always happening. The press report of my ordination began NEW MINISTER ORDAINED IN DRUMREAGH. The column beside it was headed, ATROCITY AT BENDOORAGH. Bendooragh cross is about four hundred yards from the Meetinghouse. The atrocity was that when people got up on the morning of my ordination they found that during the night all Master Adair's cows had been painted green. There was never a dull moment.

My preaching and teaching responsibilities were the Sunday Morning Service in the Church and a Bible Class on Wednesday evenings, and in Balnamore a Bible Class every Sunday afternoon and a fortnightly evening Service. The alternate 'free Sunday evening' generally was given to preaching in local schools like Cabra, Vow, Drumaheagles, and so on. I started the mid-week Bible Class in the Church and, following in my father's footsteps, believed that a Bible Class was for the study of the Bible and not for a series of perhaps interesting but unrelated talks. At the first meeting I made this clear and offered to conduct the Class on any book of the Bible they chose with one exception. Immediately, one man asked for the *Book of Revelation,* which I said was the only one on which John Calvin had not written a commentary because he did not understand it and that I was in the same position. Of course, I had read it and also R.H. Charles' learned introduction in the International Critical Commentary. But I hadn't mastered the mathematical mysticism of St. John the Divine. Simply reading it is very different from having undertaken a detailed study. The man concerned was very wrath. Indeed, so much so that I have often wondered was this because it would have provided him with an opportunity to acquaint us with his own views. However, we weathered the situation and started into a detailed study of the Catholic Epistles.

The farming folk were upright and honest. If they promised you £5 they would not offer you either £4.19.11, or £5.0.1. This gave an impression of hardness which was not really there. They did contribute generously to the Church from their meagre means. There was not much pleasure in their lives or relaxation. Though the wireless was beginning to be common and there were soirées and concerts and weekly choir-practice life was hard. The ploughing was done with horses. The cows were milked by hand. There was a lot of drudgery.

There was little drunkenness, but a considerable amount of sexual immorality. In one thing the Presbytery of Route differed from all the other presbyteries. The old Scottish Discipline (apart from the penitent having to sit on the penitent's stool) was still followed. Its application now had been reduced to cases of sexual offences. This was accepted by the community. A married couple, or a single girl, voluntarily appeared before the Kirk Session confessing their 'sin', asking the Session for absolution and to be restored to Christian privileges and for the child to be baptised. The Session's approach while firm was not so harsh as some writers have tried to make out. Further, the Session could at times show great sympathy and understanding.

The people of Balnamore were different from the farming community. One old lady used to tick me off when I visited for my smoking and sinfulness. Then one evening I received a phone call from the Route Hospital to say that she was there and that she had been badly burned. Thinking that she had scalded herself or that she had fallen into the fire, I went straight away to see her to find that she had set fire to the bed clothes when smoking in bed. She never mentioned smoking to me afterwards.

Let me end where I probably should have begun — with the Rev. Samuel Wallace. He was a model senior minister and with him I had the happiest of relationships. He was full of humour. On one occasion he was listening to the Rev. J.B. Armour and the Rev. John Waddell chatting about a certain person when Armour said "You know he hasn't spoken to me for ten years" and Waddell remarked "he hasn't spoken to me for twenty". When like a flash came the observation, "Mr Armour, you have a grievance". He taught me many things without my knowing I was being taught. One day I met him coming from the Route Hospital. After a short chat he said:

"Barkley, when you are visiting a woman in hospital ask her if it's an appendix and if not ask her no more questions".

Wise counsel, which I observed all my life. An opportunity to speak has been offered. It may be taken up. It may not. The important thing is that without embarrassment an opportunity to speak has been given.

He could read people like a book. On one occasion a neighbouring minister was seeking to find out how we were getting on together, and tried the ploy of asking:

"Did you hear a good sermon yesterday Mr Wallace?"

The reply was:

"I heard a couple of good ones on the wireless and I saw Barkley, I saw Barkley".

Mr. Wallace was hard of hearing. I prefer that to saying he was deaf, because if anyone (including myself) missed out anything he always heard the omission. Politically, he was a Gladstonian liberal and knew as a presbyterian farmer's son that it was the Liberals who had made them free men, by which I mean that while many Liberals, following the 1885 General Election, formed the Ulster Liberal Unionist Association he accepted the Route Tenants Defence Association's declaration of confidence in Gladstone. He could sit for hours talking about Parnell, Butt and Redmond.

Theologically he approached problems with an open mind, and in conducting public worship and celebrating the Sacraments used *The Euchologion,* the epoch making Service Book of the Church Service Society in Scotland, first published in 1867. I inherited his copy. He was wary of the supra-religious, who added their own requirements for salvation to those set forth in the Scriptures by Christ so that they no longer really worshipped Christ so much as their own ideas. On one occasion when I was visiting Mr Wallace one of these quasi-religious called, and during our conversation asked:

"Our church is vacant. Could you recommend me a good minister who doesn't smoke?"

Like lightning, in his squealy voice, came the answer:

"No, but I could recommend you a dozen who do".

He was grim in appearance until you saw the ever twinkling eyes. He was full of wit. He was a man of integrity, justice and goodwill.

God was extremely good to me to give me such a man, as senior minister, in my first congregation. I owe more than I can say to him.

An important event in my life at this time, one which was to have consequences through ups and downs for over fifty years, was my marriage in1936 to Irene Graham, daughter of the Rev. Robert Anderson of Richview and Esther Price Kertland, daughter of the Rev.W.J. Kertland of Second Waterford. The latter had been Chaplain to Spike Island and became a presbyterian by conviction. Irene was born in Castlewellan but had become acclimatised to city ways rather than those of the countryside. In Richview, she was a Sunday-School teacher and also founded and ran a Girls' Club. It is funny sometimes how events follow a particular pattern. I did not apply for any of the congregations of which I was minister. In each case, I was called, as it were, out of the blue. Even so, they had one common feature with only slight variations. When I went to Drumreagh, it had not had a minister's wife for over fifty years; in Second Ballybay and Rockcorry, Harry Boyd had for fifteen years been a bachelor and he was succeeded by my friend Robin Wilson who was only married one year when he left. And in Cooke Centenary, Cassells Cordner after fifteen years as a bachelor married and retired two years later.

Sometimes I joked about this, saying that the congregations were obviously looking for a minister's wife not a minister.

The role of the minister's wife is impossible to define. So far as Irene was concerned she had a free hand and was not tied to any tradition by the immediate past. At that time, in some congregations, the minister's wife was treated as if she were an unpaid curate. While those of my day regarded this not only as unfair but as unjust, there was not one of us who would have submitted his wife to being brought in and questioned by a hearing committee or session before the congregation had made out a Call.

Irene was musical and a gifted pianist. This was a natural talent rather than an accomplishment. She never would have doubled a major third though, if you asked her why, she possibly could not have told you. Her playing was instinctive in its execution and quality. When I went to Drumreagh, Thomas Fulton was precentor and there was a good choir who met every Thursday with their tonic-solfa and they doh-ray-me'd and lah-te-doh'd the tunes of the Psalter. I enjoyed the tonic as I had learned it at school. Eventually an organ was introduced and also hymnody. Irene became organist. Personally, I prefer unaccompanied singing but for this a good choir is most necessary. Public worship is always enriched by good congregational singing and it was a joy to have it led by Drumreagh choir.

Ballybay was very different. Instead of being in the country the Manse was within a quarter of a mile of the town. It had originally been built as a Presbytery, but being about 100 yards outside the parish boundary the priest was not allowed to live in it, and the presbyterians bought it for a Manse. Being in a town there was considerably more social life than in Drumreagh. Having had no minister's wife for so long the ladies of Ballybay, and Rockcorry also, were a well-organised unit into which Irene was welcome.

Musically, north Antrim and Co. Monaghan are as far removed from each other as are the north and south poles. Second Ballybay had a pipe organ, a choir, and sang hymns. Rockcorry, on the other hand, had Alby Forster as precentor no choir and only sang psalms and paraphrases. Neither congregation had many singers. Sadly, Alby had to have an operation on his throat and this created a crisis. The Session met and, I assume because I was the only person who joined in with Alby regularly and in spite of all my protestation, they appointed me to raise the singing. Having no tuning-fork, my problem was to find the right pitch and not be too high or too low. Having been limited to Jackson, Irish, Palestrina, St Paul, St John, Wareham and Luther's Hymn for four Sundays, on the fifth, as I walked up the aisle to the pulpit, Willie Forster the Session clerk, tapped me on the shoulder and said:

"Please call a meeting of Session at the close of the Service".

I did so, opened the meeting with prayer and turned to Willie. "Your reverence," he said, "some of us have been thinkin'... "

He stopped.

"Well, Willie," I said, to get him started again, "that's nothing new". "Not only have we been thinking," he continued, "some of us have been talking."

Of course, I knew this for the previous day had been the fair and everything in the countryside, if not the world, was discussed. So I asked what had been talked about.

"Well, we were thinking that after listening to you raising the singing over the past month, we'd have to get an organ".

This was said with a beaming smile and a rare twinkle in his eye. The Session decided to introduce an organ. Again, Irene became organist.

Marriage, like many other experiences, influences one's whole life. It establishes not simply one but a whole series of new relationships and alters others. It changes one's outlook on many issues and leads to many qualifications and modifications of one's opinions on a whole variety of subjects. It teaches one many things about personal attitudes, patience, compromise, integrity, wit and humour. It widens one's ability and shows the need for empathy in the pastoral counselling of others. It reveals the need for respect and privacy. I believe everyone is entitled to that.

There were grey patches in our marriage. At the same time, I know that our difficulties were not unique. A clerical marriage, by its nature, is subject to many kinds of stresses. It is right, therefore, that I should warmly welcome both the founding of organisations like RELATE and the fact that today the Church makes provision to help not only ministers, but also minister's wives, to cope with the daily and unexpected problems that arise from time to time in a Manse and in a congregation.

4 Across the borders

In Malin they used to say to my father, "There's great air here.", to which he added, "Yes, but they expect me to live on it." I found myself in a somewhat similar position in Drumreagh in 1939, when the committee refused to pay me a bequest which was rightfully mine. This seemed very unfair to me, and I was particularly hurt and disillusioned by the fact that, when the matter was discussed, no-one had spoken out on my behalf.

The year before, the Presbytery of Route had nominated me to be a member of my first Assembly's committee — the Sustenation Fund, which deals with minister's livelihoods. By one of those strange coincidences, it was to meet the following day at noon. When the meeting concluded, I went to the War Memorial Hostel for lunch and who was there but my old pal, Bill Haslett. While chatting, he remarked: "John, there's a great vacancy down our way. Would you be interested?"

Still reeling from the day before, I said that I'd go to Australia. He told me that the candidate who was to preach on Sunday had let them down and, if I came to preach, Bill would get them to consider me at a meeting the next Monday.

I went all the way to Ballybay in Monaghan and was called. In a way, I hated to be leaving Drumreagh but there did seem to be some providential reason behind events what with meeting Bill in the circumstances I did.

On 4 May, 1939, I was installed in Second Ballybay by the Presbytery of Monaghan. I was also appointed minister-in-charge of Rockcorry.

The first presbyterian congregation in Ballybay was established in 1690-91 with the Rev. Humphrey Thompson, who preached in Irish and English on alternate Sundays, as minister. The Meetinghouse was one mile out of the town in accordance with the restrictive laws against Dissenters. Some families in Ballydian, Drumskelt, and Shantonagh, still live in the houses built in 1690-91.

Rockcorry was about ten miles from Ballybay. It had been founded around 1815 by the Rev. Samuel Moore, who was also a medical doctor, and had largely built and paid for the church. It was a friendly wee church seating about eighty people.

Second Ballybay, built in the town in 1834, is a barn church with a gallery at the back, seating 560 people. It had been a full church. James Corrie told me how he and Samuel Carlisle were married in the same week and how both of them applied to the Session for a seat. There was only one unoccupied seat in the Church and the Session gave "the second seat on the right of the gallery" to both of them "the one who filled it first to get keeping it". There James sat week after week beaming down at me, having assured me not to worry if I saw him looking at his watch unless I saw him putting it to his ear and shaking it.

Ballybay was very different from Drumreagh. It was much more relaxed. There was not the same need for conformity. While in Drumreagh pastoral visitation was a duty and a very solemn affair, in Ballybay it was much more free and easy. In Drumreagh if you weren't visiting you weren't working. In Ballybay you could be rising from a meal when someone would call saying, "There's a good football match in Oriel Park between Dundalk and Bohemians, would you like to go?", or "We're going out to shoot foxes would you like to get the rifle and join us?" The main thing in Ballybay was to keep the Manse door open, or, in other words, to be available. So far as visiting was concerned it was an opportunity for friendship and pleasure. As I said about my moulding in Magee College, visiting was enjoying what one was doing. There were possibly several reasons for this. In Drumreagh presbyterians were, at least 90% of the community, whereas in Ballybay they were under 10%. In Drumreagh, all the people were of Scottish presbyterian stock, whereas in Ballybay, at least, one third were Huguenot. Common names in the area were Bodel, Mackerel, Souter, Draffin, Breakey, Hillis, Curlew, and so on. Indeed, two of the Breakey descendants became Moderators of the General Assembly. Some histories refer to a Huguenot settlement at Castleblayney. I was not able to trace a single Huguenot name there, so I think it must refer to the Ballybay and Newbliss areas, Castleblayney being the postal town. In many homes New York, Washington, Philadelphia, and Los Angeles were better known than Dublin or Belfast. This was because of friends who had emigrated. Indeed, some had never been in the latter.

However, there were limits to this breadth of outlook. You did have the odd one like Sam Manson, who had been born in Glasgow, was brought to the county Cavan when four years of age, went to Cootehill on business, attended Rockcorry Church, but had never been in Ballybay in his life, and on his death bed asked me:

"Is Ballybay as big as Glasgow?"

One day in Hall Street National School, which had fifty or sixty children on the roll, I asked how many of them had ever seen the sea. None. So, the next Sunday School excursion went to Blackrock, Co. Louth. The youngsters had a great time. Another feature was that in Drumreagh most of the young people remained in the congregation, whereas in Ballybay most of the youngsters were 'born for export'. Some boys remained on the farm, but while there might be some thirty girls at the National School once they left they went off to be nurses, typists, stenographers, teachers, book keepers, and so on, with the result that it was possible to arrange activities for boys and young men, whereas with girls one was working with single figures. One could have a healthy Junior Girls' Auxiliary of about twenty-five, but a Senior GA was an impossibility. The benefit was that there was much more contact with the outside world when they all came home for the holidays.

Let me illustrate this from Alec Draffin's family. They had three daughters, one of whom was in America and one in England, and six sons John, Herbert, David, Eric, William and Walter. On 21 acres all were educated — John to become chief dispensing chemist in Steven's Hospital in Dublin, Herbert a surgeon in Manchester Royal Infirmary, David a professor of medicine in Newcastle, and Eric a dentist in

Harley Street. Every year as Dada and Mama were getting on in years all four of them took their holidays at the sowing and the harvest to work on the farm. David was taken prisoner-of-war at Dunkirk. I was the first to get news of this, and went out to break the news. That he was alive brought great rejoicing in Cornanure that night. David was now unable to come home for the harvest work, so in the spring and autumn each year there now came a large cheque from the War Office to pay for a man to do his share of the work. To fit in with these patterns we moved the spring communion to Easter Day, so that all the young people on holiday could sit at the Lord's Table with their parents.

I must refer to two events in 1940 which made big changes in my life. The first was the only really unpleasant thing to happen during my time in Ballybay. Fortunately, I had been minister for about a year and so was known, otherwise my ministry could have been completely destroyed. It certainly was not helped. It was so serious it cannot be ignored, so I will set it out here without comment.

A neighbouring minister (now dead) told a member of his congregation that I had used insulting language about a child in the Sunday School; he in turn told it to the child's father. It was several days before I heard about it. When I did I, quite truthfully, denied it and went to see the child's father and mother but was not received. When the said minister heard that I had denied it, he said that another minister had heard me also. This other minister on being interviewed, unknown to me, assured his interviewers that I had never used the words. Several people attempted to resolve the matter. I received a letter from a well known public figure asking:

"Would you be good enough to allow some of us to visit you in your Manse with a view to getting the matter cleared up."

I replied in the affirmative. A week later I received another letter saying "I had a letter from (naming the minister) this morning saying that our meeting is off..."

I have never discussed this with anyone and can only assume that the minister responsible had refused to come. It was fortunate, as I have said, that I had been there for twelve months, that people knew me and that the majority accepted my integrity. This experience of trust gave me faith and hope.

The second event is very different. I had had a letter from my mother saying that my father was not at all well so I went to Derry to see him. When there he asked me to go and visit Mrs Baird, of 6 Brandywell Avenue, as he was not fit to go. She was on the Communicants' Roll of Claremont Church, and a widow who lived alone. I had visited her in the past and the routine was that one knocked the door and lifted the latch and entered. It was the 2nd of May. When I returned home I told my father that she was very ill and that I thought she was dying. Two days later, my father asked me to go over and see her again. I did so, but when I knocked and tried the latch the door was locked. So I knocked again a bit louder. This brought a neighbour to the door. In a quite unfriendly tone of voice she asked:

"Are you looking for Mrs Baird?"

On my saying that I was she said, "She was buried yesterday". "But she couldn't", I replied, "she was a member of my father's congregation".

"She became a Catholic before she died and Fr. — buried her".

The details in the City Cemetery Register are:

Entry No.7291; Isabella Baird (Mrs), 6, Brandywell Avenue; died 2nd May, 1940; aged 68 years; buried 3rd May, 1940; 'in the RC plot'.

I had never come across so appalling an action in my life. I did not think anyone (especially a priest who is supposed to be an educated man) in the twentieth century could act in such a way against an old dying woman. As I mentioned, I had largely ceased to be interested in academic study following my disappointing degree result. Mrs Baird's burial altered this. I decided to resume my studies. My aim was to achieve an inter-church relationship which would make such actions impossible, and to do this by scholarship and learning, not polemical confrontation. This was to have far-reaching consequences for me.

I wrote to Trinity College for permission to enrol as a research student for the degree of Doctor of Philosophy on the subject of Probabilism. TCD replied that they could not enrol a student for two degrees at the same time and that if I wished to do so I would have to surrender the two parts in which I had already passed in the Bachelor of Divinity examination. It was a case of 'No Surrender'.

There was too much presbyterian stubbornness in me to do that. So I completed my BD, pursuing the moral question as a private study.

I was able to trace this back through Alphosus Liguori to the Dominican Bartholomew Medina (1527-81) at Salamanca whose views were developed by the Jesuits: "If the licitness or illicitness of an action is in doubt, it is lawful to follow a probable opinion favouring liberty, even though the opposing opinion, favouring the law, is more probable". It was the Jesuits pleading of this defence which led Blaise Pascal in his *Provincial Letters* to ask, "Are they Christians or Turks — men or demons?" While my survey may need further development, it is to be hoped that the Ecumenical Movement has completely brought to an end such behaviour between the Churches in Ireland.

I mention this here because the quietness of my life in Ballybay allowed me to study, as and when I was able, for the next nine years.

Without being a bookworm, I was fairly widely read but this fortunately convinced me that while I had accumulated a considerable amount of knowledge on a variety of subjects much of it had not been inwardly digested and made mine. This applied to questions like natural and revealed religion, moral bases, authority and experience, means and ends, immortality and resurrection, preaching and eucharist, ecclesiology and creeds, history and eternity, and others. Not merely reading, but studying and mastering was needed. These ten years were to lay the foundations for the rest of my life.

The BD examination in TCD consisted of four compulsory parts — Old Testament, New Testament, Dogmatics, and Church History — two optionals, and an extra examination required for all non-Anglicans. Of the optionals I took Philosophy of Religion and Liturgics. These studies taught me to seek the abundant riches of the New Testament, and avoid particular dogmatic theories.

In 1940 I applied to Dublin University for permission to enrol as a research student for the degree of Doctor of Philosophy, not in moral philosophy, as I had intended, but on "Christian Worship: The Heart of the Christian Life". The title is based on a statement by Professor H. Lietzmann in *The Founding of the Church Universal,* where he says, "The heart of the Christian life is to be found in the act of public worship". The thesis began with a detailed study of the Jewish background and agreed with the conclusion of Nielen that:

whenever we find in primitive Christianity elements cognate with Judaism, they are to be assigned, unless specifically and explicitly Christian, to Jewish influence ... Jewish influence is to be assumed where all other explanations leave us unsatisfied.

This was followed by a study of the New Testament data in the light of the Jewish background. Here it was found that the Christian ecclesia took over the form of worship of the Jewish synagogue, but filled it with a new spirit, placing the emphasis on the revelation of God in Christ. The Gospel replaced the Torah as the definitive reading. So arose the Liturgy of the Word, which was open to all, believers, catechumens, hearers, and so on.

The Christian Church in the earliest days, also, continued the Jewish practice of the *Haburah,* or religious meal, but the bread with which the formal part of the meal commenced and the Cup of Blessing with which it ended were interpreted in the light of the prophetic words and actions of Jesus at the Last Supper and of the Passion and Resurrection. So arose the Eucharist-*Agape,* to which believers only were admitted. It was not open to all, only to members of the brotherhood or fellowship.

Later for reasons lost in the mists of history, but probably 'unworthy abuses' (I Cor.xi, 23-34) or persecution, the eucharistic bread and wine came to be separated from the social meal. So arose a distinction between Eucharist and *Agape,* and the former was united with the Liturgy of the Word to form a unity. Thus there came into being the classical structure of the Liturgy. The rite is a unity, even though it is possible to separate the various elements for study purposes. The Liturgy of the Word consists of praise, prayer, Scripture readings and exposition. The sacramental meal consists of four actions within a unity — offertory, consecration, manual actions (breaking bread and taking cup), and communion of the people. The rite is a corporate action.

I am not interested in the *anathemas* of Nicaea or Trent or Dort, but rather in the Christ whom men and women meet face to face in worship. The Eucharist or Supper in the early Church was an Easter celebration whereas an examination of the Roman Mass prior to 1965 and some reformed Protestant rites, to use the Swedish scholar Brilioth's phrase, shows they tend "to give to the sacred rite the one-sided character of a commemoration of Good Friday". The Christ, whom the people meet, is the dying, not the Risen and Triumphant Christ. This ought not to be. They should meet face to face with the Crucified and Risen Christ. In the Eastern, Western, Lutheran, Anglican and Reformed rites the ideal is weekly communion. Karl Barth declared:

Worship without the Eucharist is a theological impossibility and... we have not received from God the right to make this liturgical amputation, we have usurped it.

It was the civil authority which prevented Calvin holding weekly communion in Geneva. How he solved the problem was not by drawing up a separate Sunday Morning Service, but by taking the Service for the Sacrament of the Lord's Supper and rubricating it as to how it should end if there was no actual celebration of the Supper. In other words, the norm was the Liturgy of the Word, not an Anglican Quire Office or an Independent compilation.

I firmly believe that there should be a more frequent celebration than is normal in Irish Presbyterianism today. This is not simply on historical or theoretical grounds, for a means of grace should not be assessed that way. It arises from pastoral reality. When I was minister in Cooke Centenary there was a home in which the father and mother had begun court proceedings and filed papers for divorce. It was possible to effect a reconciliation but I was faced with a frightful problem, They said that they wished to renew their vows to each other at the Lord's Table. Holy Communion had been celebrated two days before and there would not be another for three months. Had we had Communion monthly it might have been possible to make arrangements for three weeks hence. But three months! "You shall not renew your vows to each other for three months"!

I would like to see at least a monthly communion. Tommy Toye could observe the practice in nineteenth century Belfast without any difficulty or problem. Pastorally, I believe it to be necessary today.

Out of my studies came ten conclusions: that God must be worshipped, that Christian unity can only be achieved through joint worship, that Christ died for all, that the initiative is divine, that while worship must be relevant there is no place for stunts to attract, that Christian theology is a system in which doctrines are inter-related, that there should be frequent celebration of holy communion, that worship is corporate action minister and people participating in a unity, that renewal grows out of the past in ecumenical perspective, and that a rigid dogmatic structure is not a necessity. These became a part of what I am.

There was another factor of great significance surrounding the writing of this thesis. Dr. J.E.L. Oulton, Regius Professor of Divinity, was my supervisor. I went to Dublin for a full week each term, where he interviewed me and I had all the facilties of the Library to consult rare texts. Between visits I prepared part of a chapter and left it with him, discussing what I had left on the previous occasion. The interviews were very thorough and being a distinguished patristic scholar he always quoted the Fathers in Latin or Greek while I searched for a phrase or word to provide a clue as to whether it was Ignatius or Cyril of Jerusalem, Tertullian or Cyprian, to whom he was referring. This emphasis on checking the texts of primary sources has never left me.

However, I learned much more than that. In the section of the thesis dealing with the origins of the Roman and Gallican rites I followed the findings of the French Benedictines, Cabrol and Le Clerc, rather than those of Mgr Louis Duchesne. On reading over what I had prepared to hand in the next day, it suddenly dawned on me that Dr. Oulton had written an article on this very subject in W.A. Phillips' *History of the Church of Ireland.* So I looked it up to find that he had taken the same view as Duchesne. It was now 12.30 am and my train was at 9.15 in the morning so nothing could be done. On the train I decided the proper thing to do was to tell him. He asked:

"Did you state your reasons?"

I said I had given eight pages of reasons. He then said:

"Barkley you are a research student. If you give your reasons and they are sound you do not need to agree with me in anything".

This did not prevent him writing to me later to ask if I knew that Le Clerc had said, "These two rites differ as do two different races of men". I replied that I did but Le Clerc's statement was based on a comparison of fourth and fifth century Roman manuscripts with seventh and eighth century Gallican. We also differed in our interpretation of the 1552 *Book of Common Prayer,* where he accepted the traditional Anglican view whereas I held with Dom Gregory Dix that it was 'zwinglian'. My one hope is that I have always adopted the same objective attitude so far as any of my students were concerned. Dr. Oulton contributed not a little to what I am.

"Tell it not in Gath, publish it not in the streets of Ashkelon", neither let it be known in Church House, "lest the daughters of the Philistines rejoice". When this thesis had been completed I, in my pride, would have said that I could answer any question I was asked about the great Eastern liturgies. About twelve months later, I was in London on the Lord's Day and I decided to go to the Greek Cathedral of St. Sophia in Moscow Road where the Liturgy of St. Chrysostom was being celebrated. Then I realised that I really knew nothing about it. Oh! I knew the facts. I knew the structures. But I knew nothing of the mysticism, majesty and glorious melody in Orthodox worship of the unaccompanied songs of praise to God. Here I discovered in a new way that worship cannot be fully understood with the mind, but must be experienced. In the Cathedral of St. Sophia, I learned never to despise the worship of others.

Having been awarded a Doctorate in Philosophy, I continued my liturgical studies and wrote a thesis on "The Eucharistic Rite in the Liturgy of the Church of Scotland" and submitted it for the degree of Doctor of Divinity. I had written a brief dissertation on this for the Bachelor of Divinity degree and my Ph.D. thesis supplied an extensive background. I had discovered that in all Zwingli wrote about the Lord's Supper in spite of his radical approach to the rite the question of Christ's 'spiritual' presence with His people was never in dispute. What was in dispute was the sense in which Christians might say, as Zwingli repeatedly said, that in the Supper they do 'truly' feed on the body and blood of the Lord. Zwingli holds without equivocation "Christ is the host and also the food" (*hospes et epulum*). Zwingli is frequently accused of believing in "a mere commemoration". He holds the feeding is spiritual, sacramental or symbolic, and consists essentially in trusting in the Christ who died and rose again for us men and our salvation. Calvin's doctrine is frequently said to be superior to Zwingli's simply because Calvin puts a greater emphasis on the description of the rite as "eating and drinking" rather than Zwingli's "trusting and being reassured". "On the positive affirmation that mattered most", writes C.J. Cadoux, "there was nothing to choose between the two great Swiss reformers!" Further, I found myself in agreement with Barclay in his *Protestant Doctrine of the Lord's Supper,* where he says, 'While in these latter days, Lutheran, Zwinglian,and Calvinist differ widely in their Eucharistic doctrine, such divergences were not so marked in those whom they acknowledge as their spiritual fathers, for in their essential teaching on the Holy Supper, Luther, Zwingli, and Calvin are one'.

Reformed theology rejects both 'zwinglianism' and 'transubstantiation'. To quote the *Scots Confession* of 1560:

In the Supper rightly used, Christ Jesus is so joined with us, that he becomes very nourishment and food of our souls. Not that we imagine any transubstantiation of bread into Christ's body, and of wine into his natural blood.. Whosoever slanders us, as that we affirm or believe Sacraments to be naked and bare Signs, do injury unto us, and speaks against the manifest truth... We will neither worship the Signs, in place of that which is signified by them, neither yet do we dispise, and interpret them as unprofitable and vain, but do use them with all reverence

It is my opinion, therefore, that if any minister distributes the consecrated Bread saying, "This is the body of Christ... ", and the Cup saying, "This cup is the new covenant in the blood of Christ", but meaning in his heart, "They are not. They are only empty symbols", he should resign immediately. Definition is impossible. Descriptions and illustrations are inadequate and limited. But a thing does not need to be 'material' to be 'real', and it is possible by faith to partake of the body and blood of Christ. The Table is the Table of the Lord, not of a denomination.

Following the conferring of the DD degree both Dr. E.H. Alton, Provost, and Dr. Oulton, asked me if possible to publish. I applied to several reputable publishers. One of them replied that, though they had received very favourable learned reports upon it, it could not be published without a subsidy.

The Ulster Bank was agreeable to increasing my overdraft by £500, but, though I applied to several trusts and members of the church I was unable to get a loan of the rest. So it was never published. This at the time was a bitter disappointment. To do so today would be a work of pseudo-supererogation.

So much for my intellectual development, such as it was, in the years 1940-50. I may have been bit of late developer or something, but I greatly matured as a result of the studies undertaken during those years. I was also much more adequately equipped for my calling as a minister of Christ.

In the sphere of pastoral ministry, I cannot adequately pay tribute to my Session Clerk, Alex Brown, and his wife and family for their friendship, and the leadership they offered the congregation. They really were an Aaren and Hur to me. My visiting duties were always a great pleasure. All my members in both Ballybay and Rockcorry were farmers. Some had shops, but they also farmed. The farmer's life was ploughing and sowing, harrowing, digging turf, cutting hay, reaping corn and barley, and digging and pitting the potatoes. My visiting routine therefore fell into a pattern. From 31 October to Christmas visit Ballybay. From February 1st to St. Patrick's Day visit Rockcorry. Three visits three days per week, except Drumgoole and Drumruhill when there were five. Provided one visited the sick diligently there was plenty of time for study, fishing, and shooting without one's pastoral work suffering.

Owing to wartime petrol rationing most of my visiting had to be done by bicycle, or taking the car to a house and continuing on foot over the fields and along the loanings. Each visit lasted from two to three hours. When visiting Rockcorry if the car was not working I simply went down to the railway station and Dan the guard said, "Where are you for today?" and the train stopped and let me off. "At whose house will you be at when we're coming back?" "Will you be coming back on the afternoon or evening train?" I told Dan, and the train stopped to pick me up, or blew its whistle if I were not at the side of the line. Sometimes I went in the guard's van, on others I rode on the plate, changed the staff at Shantonagh, and fulfilled a boyhood dream to be an engine driver. Perhaps the house I was for was in Co. Cavan and I went and borrowed Willie Forster's boat to row across the river or perhaps across the lake. It was real life. The first part of a visit could consist in stooking corn, shooting rabbits, doing a while's fishing, or chatting, according to circumstances. One year I arrived at Mrs Hillis' when she was sending off her hens to Cork to participate in the Irish egg-laying competitions. I helped her to catch and box them. She won first prize. Each year after that she waited, if possible, for my visit to catch them and send them off.

Or Jack Mehaffey, whom I don't think had ever shaved in his life, and, though in his seventies, was as hardy as a wild-duck. He seldom came to church, but every year gave me the present of a pike when I visited. This year I announced that I would visit Clossiaghmore on a Monday. We had a great old yarn and after I had had a big meal in his brother Willie's and prayed, out we went to the car. Jack stood on one foot and then on the other and seemed most uneasy. When I switched on the engine he could stand it no longer and ran off shouting, "Wait a minute". When he came back he handed me a pike saying:

"Never visit Clossiaghmore on a Monday again for I had to go out and break the Sabbath yesterday to have this for you".

Often the house to house visitation was supplemented by putting on one's Wellingtons and going through the fair or attending a ploughing match. I could reminisce for a week, but I will just mention a few instances that will well illustrate the character of the people.

Samuel Robert Scott of the townland of Aghakist typifies much of the Ulster Presbyterian character. After I had been in Ballybay about three years, one day when I was visiting he said to me:

"Mr Barkley I want to tell you I did not sign your Call".

When I replied that I didn't know, he continued:

"Have you not got the Call?"

I said I had.

"Well, did you not read the names on it?"

"No", I said, for I had made a point of not doing so.

"You were quite entitled not to sign it. It does not matter who signs it so long as they give one a chance to prove that he is at least half as good as the man they voted for. So forget about the whole thing".

"But", he said, "I can't".

I again asked him to drop the subject. Then he exploded.

"I just want to tell you I was wrong".

There the matter ended, but I saw in it what I felt to be the honour and integrity of the Ulster character.

The post mistress was Miss Bulfin, a member of the Roman Catholic Church. I had a widow, Mrs Williamson, who lived alone at Swann's Cross. She had a son Archie working away from home. This day Richie Gilliland arrived at the door to say Miss Bulfin would like me to call into the Office as soon as possible. So I went down at once. It was to tell me that Archie had been killed in an accident and she did not want to send out the telegram to his mother in case she was alone in the house. Could I go out and be there when it arrived? Needless to say I was, but it was thanks to Miss Bulfin's thoughtfulness.

I should also mention the first time I visited Nat, who lived in the heart of Corfinlough bog, I did not know what I was in for. We weren't long chatting until the name of Dean Swift arose and I found myself in the presence of a man who had read everything Swift had ever written, and a vast number of books about him. His views on Jonathan, Stella, and Vanessa were stimulating and enthralling. One was right back in the eighteenth century with its culture, intrigues, poverty, pseudo-refinements, and sin. The result was that every year the night before I visited Corfinlough I had to refresh my scant knowledge of the Dean. I was honoured to sit at the feet of this solid Ulster farmer, widely read and worthy of academic distinction though he had never been anywhere but at a National School.

Or let me take the case of George. He was a farmer and owned a scutch mill, a good footballer and determined full-back. He belonged to a neighbouring congregation, not mine, but I knew him well as I had been there about seven years. It was a Monday I am almost certain in February 1946 when he called asking me for a Letter of Introduction as he was emigrating. He was the sort of lad — bright and jolly, full of fun and wit, open and friendly, kind and upright — that one would have expected, as I did, to be at church every Sunday. Why, I know not, I asked him:

"Had you a good sermon yesterday?"

"I never go to Church".

I was shaken and astonished. I really did not know what to say for it was the last answer I expected. When I asked why, George's answer ran something like:

"The first Sunday I went to hear that new minister preach he quoted *Ivanhoe* and said it was *Rob Roy*. A man who could misquote Sir Walter Scott could misquote the Bible and mislead you. So I never go".

One never knows the accomplishments and distinctions a minister may meet in visiting, or how he himself may be enriched. Nor does he know who may be in his congregation.

Then there was the case of Long Willie English. He lived alone in Dunmaurice. This townland was always visited along with Corrush and they formed an L. I went out the Blayney Road along the foot of the L, visited Long Willie, and came back and up the side road to the top of the L, working from Hillis' down to Clarke's. It was a Monday. I went to Long Willie's, got no answer; tried the door, locked; went round the outhouses, no sign; looking at the floods in the meadow, I thought he must have had to go off to check on the flax. So, on I went. Of course, there was no getting back for I was not out of Clarke's until eleven o'clock. Seeing Long Willie in the town on Wednesday, I crossed the street to speak to him:

"I was awfully sorry to miss you on Monday".

"What do you mean, missed me?"

"When I called you weren't there".

"You never called".

"Oh! but I did".

"You never called".

"Often someone would have seen me go into your lane, but there was only a child with a tin lid on a brush handle at the cottages".

"You never called".

"I did".

"I stayed in all afternoon, and you never called".

By this time I saw it was getting serious and that Long Willie until his dying day would believe I had never called. As I left I said:

"There's one decent man ".

"What do you mean decent man?"

"Well, I said to myself, there's a decent man — he has had to go off because of the floods and he locked his dog in the barn, and a right han'lin' he was making of the bottom of the door".

He looked at me.

"That's right the dog was in the barn. You were there".

I was glad we got that sorted out, for I liked Long Willie. He had that presbyterian stubbornness but was always prepared to face facts. He is fair even if he finds it hard to alter his opinion. Long Willie had been lying asleep and did not hear me.

The P.P. and C.C. of Ballybay were Fr. Duffy and Fr. King. I was friendly with both and would at times stop for a chat in the street. The former and I, on occasion, would walk together at funerals. This was long before Vatican II so when the hearse came to the Presbyterian Church gate he said good afternoon. I did the same at the Roman Catholic Church gate. Consequently, it was disappointing when Bishop O'Callaghan at his consecration in 1946 saw fit to misrepresent and condemn the Protestants within his diocese. He accused Protestant business men of not employing Roman Catholics. I was Public Interest Agent in the Monaghan presbytery and wrote by direction to him in this capacity pointing out that in Monaghan, Castleblayney, Ballybay, Carrickmacross, Glaslough, Newbliss and Clones, there were Roman Catholics employed by Protestants, whereas the only Protestant employed by a Roman Catholic in the whole of Co. Monaghan was one boy who worked part-time as an auctioneer's clerk in Ballybay. The letter was never acknowledged, let alone answered.

Even so, it was possible to promote trust and harmony. When World War Two broke out in 1939, it was decided to set up a local branch of Muintir na Tire. So far as I remember, it was made up of five representatives of the professions, of business, of farmers, of labourers and of the unemployed, who were all elected at a public meeting. One of its tasks was to provide turf and wood for the poor. In February, going up the town, I saw a man I knew unloading wood at probably the wealthiest building in the town. My own stock was low, so I stopped and admired the big blocks, intending to order a load for myself but I was told that they were from Muintir na Tire. I said, "If you go on like this, there'll be not a stick left for the poor by St. Patrick's Day".

I carried out an enquiry and all deliveries to the patently undeserving stopped.

My intervention had two consequences. The Protestants asked what I thought I was doing getting involved in the first place. My answer was that I, like all Christians, had a social responsibility. Also, when I was at the meeting of the branch, nothing could be done behind my back. The Roman Catholic community, on the other hand, welcomed my participation. But the next year, when the professional representatives were elected, I was not one of them. However, when it came to the representatives of the unemployed,

Fred Anderson of Corrybrannon jumped up and proposed me. The chairman objected.

"You can't say that Mr. Barkley is unemployed".

But Fred was able for him.

"The unemployed do not need to be represented by one of themselves but by someone they know is able to stick up for them".

Then Hugh Connor (Hall St.) chipped in, with

"I second Fred's proposal. Sure, Barkley's the only honest man on the council".

While acknowledging Hugh's statement to be a slight exaggeration, I am proud to say that each year from that on, until I left Ballybay, I was the first nominee for the unemployed.

I was also called to act, at government level, on the question of the recognition of presbyterian marriages by the Roman Catholic Church in Éire. In February 1945 a marriage had taken place in Drogheda Presbyterian Church. It was a mixed marriage, and the bride was a minor. About a fortnight later the *Irish Press* carried a photograph showing the couple coming out of Trim Cathedral. They has just been wed, although we had already married them. This ran contrary to the constitution. However, after a lengthy correspondence, Mr. de Valéra assured the Presbytery, through me, of the validity of presbyterian marriages. A satisfactory outcome.

Another instance of discrimination involved the appointment of a teacher "for boot making and repairing" in Castleblayney. Seven of the eight applicants, all Roman Catholics, could teach "boot repairing", the other applicant, a presbyterian, was the only one of them who could teach "boot making" as well. He did not get the job. Again I wrote to de Valéra. While I did not agree with him, I had always found de Valera to be considerate and upright. This time, however the matter was not satisfactorily resolved. Rather than appoint a presbyterian, the position was left vacant.

I could reminisce for hours about these days, about the night Davy Glass was chased by his heifer; the evening Graham blew with his shotgun the peak of the master's cap; the evening Clarke's cat jumped on the red-hot range; Tom Steen and his fiddle; Mrs Caldwell pickling the trespassers with the shotgun; on and on it could go, but I will end with a most important and delightful event, the adoption of my daughter Lois on Christmas Eve, 1943. Now there was a new spate of theological questions to be answered every year. For instance, sometimes after the evening service I would take Lois for a short walk. On one occasion, when she was about six, I felt a spit of rain and said, "Put an inch to your step or we'll get wet". This was followed by a long silence, so I knew trouble was brewing.

"Daddy, does God send the rain?"

"Yes, God sends the rain".

That was easy but was followed by a longer silence. Then, out it came.

"Daddy, does God not know we're out?"

Down the years I had a lot of such questions to face.

Lois' career at the Manse was to begin with an amusing incident. There was a lady in the congregation who was great chat, but sometimes she would point out that today's ministers were not to be compared with those of former days. Her chief complaint was that they didn't read the Bible. As I mentioned, I always had a service on Christmas Day. At its close on the day following Lois' arrival she came up to me and said:

"I hear you have company at the Manse".

"Yes", I said, "we have".

"Is it a boy or a girl?"

"A girl".

"That's lovely, what are you calling her?"

"Lois".

"Lois, that's a lovely name. Isn't it French?"

"I see you don't know your Bible any better than the ministers".

Gales of laughter all round. Never after did ministers not read the Bible.

From childhood, Lois has been a real God's gift to me and a priceless blessing through days of difficulty and loneliness as well as of joy.

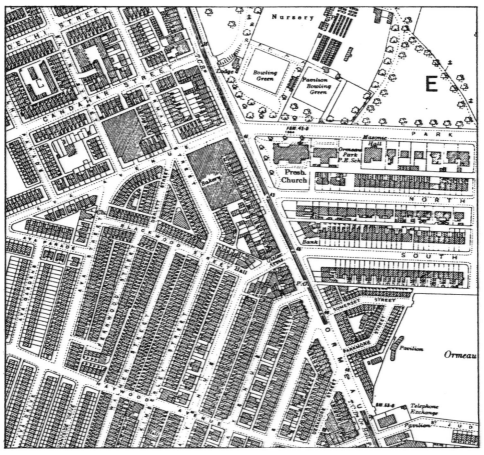

Cooke Centenary Church, Belfast.

5 Taking stands: the call to Cooke

I was happy in Ballybay and Rockcorry and had no thought of leaving, though I did have one practical problem.

Like others, whose Calls were prior to 1940, I had an overdraft. I had been brought up never to buy anything if I had not the money to pay for it. This I had tried to observe but, being on the ministerial minimum, I had had on several occasions to make adjustments. I knew that nothing was so damaging to a minister's reputation in a local community as the fact that he did not pay his bills when they were due, so all bills like groceries, milk, garage, and so on were paid monthly on the dot. Sometimes there was no money to do so and the Bank had to fill the breach. While not liking this I did not feel so bad as it could charge interest. I also knew the tragic side of the situation as on two occasions I had had to contribute (and I did so gladly, if, on the other hand, sadly) to pay for the coffin and help to clear the debts of brother ministers. How sad that this should be the position of men who had served the Church for almost forty years. Even so when faced with having to make a decision on receiving a Call from Cooke Centenary Church, Belfast, this was really only a secondary consideration — but it was a real consideration nonetheless, though the Bank held an insurance policy as security. This helped to make who and what I am as regards money. I liked my cheque when it was due, not a week or month afterwards.

When I came to Cooke, it was always handed to me on the last

Sunday of each month. This was something new. Consequently I was determined that every member on the Old Age Fund or the Orphan Society got their money on the date it was due, and from me personally, not the Deaconess or the Assistant. To handle money in Christ's name is a sacred trust.

Henry Cooke, the best known name in Irish presbyterianism, was born at Grillagh, Maghera, on 11 May, 1788. He was educated at a 'hedge-school' and Glasgow. A student for the Ministry under the care of the Presbytery of Route he was ordained in Duneane on 13 November, 1808. He was moderator of the Synod of Ulster in 1824-25, and twice of the General Assembly in 1841-42 and 1862-63. In the Arian Controversy in 1820-29, he was the Champion of Orthodoxy, and it is on this his fame principally rests, especially when it is linked with the part he played in the organising of Toryism in Belfast. Though a presbyterian and a son of the soil, Cooke opposed the Land Act as 'socialism' and his friends were the Hillsboroughs, the Rodens and the Mountcashels. Their influence encouraged him to split the Church. In a sense he was an enigma and though one may deplore some aspects of his career it would be churlish to attempt to say other than that he was the most important figure in nineteenth century Irish presbyterianism. I could not but feel myself a most unlikely heir to his mantle.

Belfast did not grow, but exploded, in the second half of the nineteenth century. The population in 1840, the year of the formation of the General Assembly, was approximately 90,000. In 1890, the year of the foundation of Cooke, it was 279,089. The first church built by the Assembly was Newtownbreda in 1842. In 1840 there were fifteen. Cooke Centenary was opened in 1890 and was the fortieth — twenty-five churches were built in fifty years or one large congregation every two years. The organisation of the congregation was sanctioned by the General Assembly in 1888. As that was the centenary of the birth of Dr. Henry Cooke, "who had done so much for Irish presbyterianism", it was decided to name the new Church at Ormeau after him. It was opened for public worship in 1892, being dedicated by the Rev. George Mathieson, D.D., Edinburgh. In the scroll over the chancel arch (now filled with organ pipes) is inscribed his text: "God is spirit. God is light. God is love".

It was a great occasion and at the festive dinner seated next to the guest preacher was President W.D. Killen. It is told, and it is possibly not all apocryphal, that Sir J.M. Barrie had published his *A Window In Thrums* in 1889 and Mathieson was full of it and turning to Killen asked him if he read it to receive the reply, "I never read fiction", to which Mathieson retorted, 'Then you never read your own books'.

The first minister was the Rev. John Macmillan, who retired in 1930, after nearly forty years service. He was succeeded by the Rev. Cassells Cordner, who was installed in 1931. He retired on 1 June, 1948. One heard more about what was going on in the Church in far off places like Ballybay, than in Belfast, so I knew that the church was vacant, that candidates had been heard, that the name of a friend of mine had been put to a congregational meeting but had not received sufficient votes to be called, that things had been said about him which, in my opinion, ought not to have been said, or at least had been said in such a way that they were misunderstood, and that "the congregational meeting had broken up in disorder". I was not to know that these events were to help to determine my future. After the meeting David Rea, elder and treasurer, was walking up the Ormeau Road with the Rev. W.R. Megaw and said to him:

"Could you recommend us a man who would restore this congregation into a Presbyterian church instead of a glorified sectarian hall?"

Why David should have used the term 'sectarian hall' I do not know. I can only guess. Cooke had become like the time of the Judges when everyone did "that which was right in his own eyes". There was no unity. An ultra-fundamentalist group ruled the Session and bossed the Minister. Most youth work had ceased to belong to the congregation because of all the restrictions imposed by the Session. The choir was divided into parties. Where there should have been friendship, brotherhood, and peace, there was little, if any, peace or goodwill. Megaw replied:

"I know of only one man, Dr. Barkley of Ballybay".

"No use", said Rea, "we want a young man".

I assume he identified being a Doctor with Dr. John Macmillan, the first minister of the congregation. Megaw then said:

"He's not old. He's only about thirty-six".

My name and address was noted. As a result I received a letter asking me if I would preach on trial for Cooke. I replied stating what I had heard and asking if it was true, and saying that if it was I was not to be considered or heard unless my friend said that he had no further interest; that if my friend did so the Session and Committee, should I get and accept a Call, would approve my inviting him as a guest preacher after I had been there about three months and pay his supply in his own congregation to enable me to be free to welcome him. Otherwise, I was not to be heard or considered. About a week later, I received a letter agreeing to what I had said and inviting me to preach on trial. I wrote thanking them for the invitation, but saying that while I held the honourable thing when preaching on trial if one was not going to accept was to withdraw before a Call is made out, in the circumstances I would not hold myself bound by this. So I preached and heard nothing for several months.

Then I was predestined (I think that is the only accurate word), one Tuesday morning in November, to drive to Monaghan and take the train to Belfast arriving at 12.05. As I left the station in Great Victoria Street a stranger spoke to me.

"Are you Dr. Barkley of Ballybay?"

When I replied that I was, he asked:

"How did you enjoy your holiday in Greystones last year?"

"What?"

He repeated the question. I replied that I never was on holiday in Greystones in my life, that I never was in Greystones except one day as a student passing through it in the train going to take a supply. Looking at me sharply, he said:

"Is that true?"

I said it was. Then he shocked me.

"I am from the Cooke Church, would you come up to my house this evening and repeat to some friends what you have told me".

I said no but asked:

"Why all the interest in Greystones?".

It turned out that my name had been discussed by the hearing committee and, at its last meeting, a Mr. N— had told how I was on holiday in Greystones last summer in a house where they had prayers every morning after breakfast, but I never went to them but sat in the lounge reading the paper and smoking my pipe. That there was a majority for calling me, but some were hesitant because of this. At this point, I said it was not proper that I should be carrying on this conversation with a member of the congregation and that I must go on to the meeting I had come to attend. However, on being asked for permission to tell members of the committee that I had said I was never in Greystones on holiday in my life I agreed that he could do so.

Later, I heard of the ingenious approach adopted. One of the hearing committee represented the youth of the congregation and at the next meeting said:

"I thought from his preaching Dr. Barkley was the right man for the youth of the congregation, but Mr N— 's comments raised certain doubts in my mind. So that there is no misunderstanding, would Mr N— repeat what he told us at the last meeting".

Mr N—, thinking he had a convert, repeated the whole thing, to be told that I had been spoken to and had said I was never on holiday in Greystones in my life. All, who were hesitant, felt that there was dirty work at the crossroads and agreed with the majority and my name was submitted to the congregation. I was called, but it was not unanimous and some eighty people walked out and held a prayer meeting during which God was specifically requested (if not ordered) to stop my coming.

The following day I received seven anonymous telegrams. "Stay where you are", "You are not a believer", "You are not saved", "Belfast doesn't need the likes of you", "You are not born again" and so on, and the following morning seventeen anonymous letters of the same ilk. I had been undecided whether or not to accept the Call, but when I got this bundle of reading I decided I must accept for if this was what passed for Christianity in Belfast they needed an evangelist there. So I accepted and was installed by the Presbytery of Belfast on 1 February 1949.

May I in passing say all anonymous letters I have ever received have been consigned to the flames except two. One was sent by an elder who continued to send one every fortnight until he died. He bought all sorts of religious papers and generally enclosed a copy of *The Revivalist* or *The British Israel Magazine* or such like. His eyesight was failing and sometimes the pamphlet had a dark purple cover and he did not see where Brown's, newsagent, Ormeau Road, had written his name and address for the delivery boy. The second has survived because of its generous introduction, "Dear Judas Iscariot... " It too was from an elder. However, thankfully, whatever one may hear, such men are not typical of holders of this office.

The prospect frightened me a bit because I had never had to look after more than one hundred and twenty or so families, I now had 760, which increased to 1128. I had had to prepare two sermons each week, but instead of preaching to one hundred and twenty people, now it was to be to 900-1000. Cooke was then one of the largest presbyterian congregations in Ireland, and I had not then to compete with TV. I had had a Bible class, but now, there were Girl Guides, Boys' Brigade, Girls' Auxiliary, a mid-week Service, a club running six nights each week, and so on. To be honest, I could never have done it had I not had my reading in Ballybay behind me, and the help and strength of Desmond Bailie and Janet Wood.

My first big shock concerned pastoral visiting. I think I can say truthfully that, prior to coming to Cooke, I had never gone to bed a single night with anyone who needed visiting not visited. In Cooke, I did between 100 and 110 visits every month, omitting July and August. Many of these were sick visits, hospital visits, or concerned with funerals, baptisms, marriages, or special problems. At the end of the first month I had about eighty not visited, I tried to catch up but at the end of the second month had one hundred and forty, at the end of the third over two hundred. It was hopeless, so I had to learn to check on those that were vital and burn the rest and begin again each month. Special and sick visits amounted to about 80-85 of the 100, so pastoral visitation amounted to twenty each for ten months or 200 per year. The assistant and deaconess did the same. Even with this highly organised system people began to complain that I was not visiting. This had to be faced, I could do no more. So I decided to announce my visiting for three days each week as it was as easy to visit announced as unannounced. *Mirabile dictu.* The criticism stopped almost at once. Apparently so long as they knew I was visiting somewhere they were quite satisfied. That, of course, is a generalization. However, it was a new experience limiting oneself to an hour instead of three on one's pastoral rounds. But 200-250 visits per year took five years to complete the whole congregation, and with the same number being done by the assistant it meant that the congregation was only fully covered once every two to three years.

While Cooke was a large congregation extending from Omagh to Ballyholme, and Lambeg to Glengormley, nine-tenths of it, at the same time, was a very compact unit from Galwally to the Ormeau Bridge and Park Road along both the Ravenhill and Ormeau Roads, with the latter solidly packed right back along the Lagan, with about forty families in the Plains and the streets off the Lower Ormeau Road. This meant that I could walk in twenty minutes from the Manse to the vast majority of the homes of the congregation. So I did nearly all my pastoral visitation on foot. This had the great advantage that I met the members of the congregation in the shops and on the streets. I was not driving past in a car, but meeting and stopping to chat. So I came to know the members of that large congregation intimately. By taking the Junior Bible Class, camping at Ganaway with 'the dandy Eighth', at least a weekly visit to the Youth Club, as well as going periodically (Christmas, Easter, day before holidays, first day after holidays) to Park Road Public Elementary School, with occasional visits to the Youth Organizations (B.B., Guides, etc.) I got to know the young people and, what is equally important, they got to know me.

Pastoral visiting, as ever, provided much fun and amusement. One Friday, as I rounded the corner of the Ormeau Bakery, I met Stanley Warnock, who told me that Tom Steen, Agra Street, was ill. This was after I had been about a year in Cooke. I looked at my watch and it was 5.10 p.m. So I said, "I'll go and see him now as I can do it before tea". When I knocked the door it was opened by a tall gaunt pale-faced man with a long beard. He looked me up and down, and said, "Come in", and turned on his heel and went into the kitchen. After we were seated he said,

"Where are you from?".

I said "The Cooke".

"Oh!", says he. "Tell me does the old boy do no visiting".

"What do you mean?"

"The old boy, does he visit none?"

"Who's the old boy?"

"Dr. Barkley. Does he visit none?"

On telling Tom I was Dr. Barkley, he did the best thing possible. He threw back his head and laughed, and we became the best of friends. While Tom belonged to Cooke, he lived with his daughter, Mrs M'Cartney, and her husband, who belonged to College Square.

After Tom died, if passing I generally called for a yarn and this was to lead me to an enriched understanding. I had noticed that there was always a vase of flowers on the kitchen table. This morning, while drinking a cup of coffee, I commented on their beauty, and Mrs M'Cartney told me the secret. It ran something like this:

"You know, Dr Barkley, you buried my father in Knockbreda, but he is not there, he is here. This is his home. He loves us. He still cares for us. So it is only his body that is in Knockbreda, his spirit and his love are here. So I never put flowers on his grave for the vandals to destroy before nightfall. Instead I place a vase of fresh flowers on the table here every Monday morning. This is where his spirit is".

Her quiet words revealed to me an enduring love and affection in the Lord.

There was a very gracious old lady in Derlett Street. She could be described as genteel and cultured, but she was also proud — so much so that it was almost impossible to help her financially though she was very needy. She would not take money. If ever there was a person sympathetic and skilled in giving help it was Mrs M'Clements, the secretary of the Benevolent Fund. Even she, however, found it impossible to solve the problem. As help was needed I, or Miss Wood, called fairly frequently. Then one night I was walking up the Ormeau Road about 2 a.m., when I suddenly had an idea. I'll put a fiver in an envelope without any name or mark and drop it through her letter-box to see what happens. It was a Friday evening. On Sunday morning she arrived at the Church and said to Mr M'Aloney, the session clerk, 'I got the Financial Report of the congregation and my name was blank so I was coming today to ask you not to print my name next year. But do you know, somebody dropped an envelope with £5 in it through my letter-box on Friday night so here is £2 for the Church'. One cannot but be touched by such people, and by their loyalty to their Church.

Because Cooke had been so good to me, I decided to retire on 30

June 1954, to enable them to call a minister before October and the beginning of the winter's work. Consequently, I preached my farewell sermon on 28 June, 1954. However, on the 29th I got a postcard giving details of a Mrs Woods, 41 Beech Street, in ward 13B in the Musgrave Park Hospital. Written across the bottom was:

"John, this woman has been in hospital for fourteen months and you have never visited her. What about it! Alfie".

I looked up my records to find that a woman of this name and address in that ward had been visited by the assistant thirteen times and twelve by myself. However, though officially retired, I went up to the hospital. Meeting a nurse, I asked for Mrs Woods.

"She's in her usual place at the far end on the left".

Having said I knew about her, I asked if there was another Mrs Woods. There was not and there never had been. So, I went down the ward and after a brief conversation asked:

"Did you hear Dr. Barkley is leaving the Cooke?"

She replied she had.

"Tell me, did he ever visit you".

"No", says she. "I'm here fourteen months and he never visited me".

There was little use trying to explain so I simply said:

"Isn't that like him. Perhaps the new man will do better".

Then there was the house at which when I called the husband opened the door and before speaking to me he shouted up the stairs:

"Darling, come down. Dr. Barkley is here to welcome us home from our honeymoon".

This shook me as there was a girl of about seventeen and a boy of about fifteen in the breakfast room. So I began to wonder was this a second marriage. However, it was a family joke. The reason was that the minister who had married them eighteen years before had promised to be at the house to welcome them home from their honeymoon, and I was the first minister they had seen since.

Finally, let me recall my first visit to Alex Clerk. It was the final visit of the day. We had had about two hours great chat, chiefly about Stormont and its political inhabitants. It was one of the most enjoyable evenings I had had for a long time. However, it had to end. So as I left, Alex said: "Thank you for your visit but I don't mind if you never come back".

Mrs Clark said, "Alex! Alex! don't say that".

However, we both laughed for all Alex meant was 'I'll see you in Church every Sunday so don't worry yourself about coming to see me'. We knew we would see each other often and gladly. He and his family were among my best friends.

Preaching is a great challenge. There were those on the Session who had criticised, quite illegally, my predecessor's sermons at Session meetings. He would try to explain. They would threaten to leave. He would plead with them not to do so. They said they needed a month to think it over. So the first item on the agenda for the next meeting was their answers. Session meetings went on to 12.30 and 12.45 a.m. In my opinion, the ringleaders turned him into a nervous wreck and caused his early death. I don't think there is anyone who is so persistent and perverse as the quasi-theologian. I was sure my turn would come. Sure enough it came at the end of two months over a quite innocuous sermon. At public worship on the Sunday there was a celebration of the Sacrament of Baptism for twins. I took as my text Genesis xxv.28: Isaac loved Esau... but Rebekah loved Jacob, and tried to show that part of the problem of Jacob and Esau began with Isaac and Rebekah, and made a plea for giving all children in a family equal opportunities.

There was a Session meeting on the Monday. It was a lovely warm spring evening. As I entered the Church grounds, I knew there was trouble for eleven men were standing in a group on the grass. one was very interested in cricket and as I passed, I said:

"Nice night that, Jack, for a game of cricket! "

"Take care you're not caught out".

This seemed to me a peculiar remark so, with foreboding, I answered:

"I'll be all right, so long as I'm not stumped".

After the meeting had been opened with prayer and the routine business conducted, we came to any other business. Immediately, Jack rose and accused me of "denying Isaac was the Lord's anointed by saying that he had favourites in his family" and if only he had been preaching the people would not have been so misled, and if I continued to preach this way he would have to have his disjunctive certificate. As moderator, I did not bother about his breach of presbyterian law, or the *non sequitur* in his argument, but simply read paragraph 155 of *The Code:*

The Kirk Session shall, on application within a reasonable time, give a certificate of disjunction to a person entitled to it. A member has a right to this certificate, if he is free from scandal, and clear so far as the congregation is concerned, of every pecuniary obligation to it into which he may have entered.

I then pointed out that, being a member of Session, his standing was beyond dispute and that, as he had asked for his disjunctive certificate, he would receive it in the following day's post. I then asked was there any further business. Eight others, each after making the apparently pre-prepared speech about my "denying that Isaac was the Lord's anointed" asked for their certificates. They were given the same assurance, and the meeting closed with prayer. Their problem was that I had not reacted like my predecessor. Several spoke to me about inviting them back. So I pointed out they were free to attend church, but that they had left the Session legally so if they wished to return to the session they would have to do so legally by being elected and installed.

All knew this to be well nigh impossible, for the following day, I received almost forty phone calls thanking me for my stand. The real problem was that Cooke was a fine congregation, but had a Session who were not in harmony with the congregation's Presbyterian ethos. This event helped to make what I am. I never fought with anyone in my life. Now I realised that at times it is necessary to stand as fast as Daniel in the lions' den. I also learned that if one is dragged into a fight and he has to take off his coat he should not put it on again until the issue is settled, care being taken that the door to friendship is never completely slammed shut.

Shortly afterwards, ten new elders were elected and ordained. Most of them were men who had been members of the congregation from early days, not co-options. Some had even been children in the Sunday School in the district before the congregation was founded. They were distinct personalities with differing gifts. They worked together as brothers. On the morning following the Princess Victoria disaster, when I went into the Session room, two elders were there before me.

"Dr. Barkley, you may need a lot of money this week and some of the elders have talked it over privately as a meeting was impossible, and we will guarantee you up to £3000".

On another occasion, in the Baptismal Service, I had introduced a congregational vow, because baptism only has meaning within 'the Household of Faith':

Do you, who now in Christ's name receive this child into the fellowship of the Church, promise, by God's help, so to order your congregational life and witness that he or she may grow up in the knowledge and love of God and be continuously surrounded by Christian example and influence?

The congregation responds "We do" and the minister says: "The Lord give you grace faithfully to fulfil these promises". This had been the practice for about two years. One week a member of the congregation who had had a son baptised the previous Sunday, was sentenced to three months in prison. At the session meeting on the Monday following, W.J. Patterson said:

"We all now take a vow at baptism. Mr N— had a child baptized two weeks ago, but was imprisoned on Friday. Should we not direct the elder for the district to visit the house weekly to see if Mrs N. needs any help?".

There was no discussion as Mr Lindsay said that he had already called on Saturday and that he would visit weekly.

As the bulk of my studies centred on the worship and practice of the Church, in my first year in Cooke, the Session agreed to having Holy Week services. They were devotional in approach, and each week night there was an attendance of 550-600. A service of Meditation and Prayer (with no preaching) was used on the Friday. On Easter Day, the Sacrament of the Lord's Supper was celebrated without tokens to enable any older people who wished to become communicants, or had lapsed, to do so and notify the minister afterwards. This continued to be the practice each year. So 1949 was the first time a Presbyterian Church in Belfast held a full series of services during Holy Week. The following year I made arrangements, but waited to see what would happen. Eventually, as Easter approached, Samuel Deans, a member from the pre-Cooke Sunday School days, recalled the services of 1949, and suggested that similar services should be held every year. This was agreed unanimously. Again, the spiritual life of the congregation was enriched.

We also had a Service of Thanksgiving on St. Patrick's Day. It also was well attended with about 400-450 present. Again, however, I should mention that we had not to compete with Coronation Street or the European Cup. We were not worried whether there was one Patrick or two and we did not argue over the views of Bury, Binchy, Carney, Beiler, O'Rahilly, and others. We knew that St. Patrick was not a Roman Catholic or an Anglican. We also knew that he was not a presbyterian. We honoured him as the Apostle of the Irish people, and as an elder stated in the Session, it was "a funny church that couldn't honour the patron Saint of the country".

While some organizations expanded, for example, Brownies from two into three groups, Guides into two companies, with a Ranger Company added, only one new organization was formed in my time. The women had their WMA's and PWA's, but there was nothing for men, so we started an indoor bowling club. This was carefully planned. It was for the men of the congregation. We did not enter any league to have half the members away one night, and on another so many visitors that our own men could not get a game. At this I felt there should be prayers, but I knew if they were at the beginning some might come in late, if at the end some might leave early. So I said nothing to see what would happen. The men themselves asked me to take prayers at nine o'clock and follow it with a cup of tea, play resuming at 9.30. This was a highly successful arrangement. I attended every Thursday night, enjoyed the bowls, and did about 60-65 visits in the process! I did not feel guilty about this because I had given up all golf, shooting, and fishing (apart from holidays) within a month of coming to Cooke. It was my one time off each week. The drawing of shots, the driving at heads, the roars of derision at misses, and slaps on the back at success helped to develop who and what I am. At this point, let me thank the men of the Cooke bowling club for their generosity in enabling me to send a parcel of goods worth about £30 to friends in the Reformed Church in Hungary every two months for over three years following the Rebellion in 1956. It was important not only to help the refugees but also to rebuild the Reformed Church within Hungary itself.

Cooke became a good Christian Session, in which no one regarded himself as spiritually superior to other members. Its attitude was co-operative and inclusive. One evening, I was visiting a charming Christian lady in her fifties and I asked her why she wasn't a communicant. She told me that she had been, but had been struck off the roll. "That's a serious matter", I said, "what happened?" Then she told me about a visit from the elder for her district, whom I knew, but was dead long before I became minister of Cooke. She had arranged to go out with a friend to the pictures and had taken a cup of tea and was washing up when there was a ring at the door. Thinking it was her friend she went down the hall smoking a cigarette with the cup and tea-towel in her hand. When she opened the door it was the district elder holding out her token, but when he saw her he withdrew it and said, "No one who smokes gets a token". From that day, twenty years before, she had never been at the Lord's Table though she wanted to be. The elder had no right to do what he did: he had no authority from the Session and had completely forgotten that Jesus Christ instituted the Lord's Supper as a means of grace for sinful men and women. He failed to see that he with his judgmental attitude was like the Pharisee in the Temple.

The elders in Cooke during my ministry were men of integrity and knew that the authority lay in the Court, not the individual. The amount of work and visiting they did was enormous. All duties and responsibilities were fulfilled as brothers. In the Session restructuring, it was decided that two of the finest elders I ever knew, Stanley Warnock and Hugh Lusk, should not be assigned districts but appointed to visit new families. Their work, skill, and fidelity in building up the congregation is beyond description.

In addition to my pastoral responsibility, the Education Board nominated me as a lecturer in Biblical Studies in Stranmillis College and in Church History in Queen's University.

In these classes, I had an interesting experience as the result of a story (perhaps apocryphal) going the rounds when I was a student in TCD. It was about two brothers, who were identical twins, who had been failed in their honours degree examination because they had copied. However, they had been able to convince the University authorities of the possibility of their innocence to the extent that they were given a re-examination. One sat this in the Examination Hall and the other in a completely separate building, Regent House. Their

Father and mother:
Robert James Barkley,
and Mary Darcus Monteith.

Malin Meetinghouse on the shores of Trawbreaga Bay, overlooking Doagh Island.
Discriminatory laws restricted the building of Meetinghouses in Ireland, so Malin
was built on sand on the foreshore which belonged to no-one. Below: Lois

Drumreagh, County Antrim.
The Meetinghouse at the Cross
(with thanks to Mr. S.A. Blair).
Below: Ordination. John Barkley
(the young, slimline version!)
with Drumreagh's Senior Minister
the Rev. Samuel Wallace,
and bicycle. (From an old
newspaper cutting.)

Second Ballybay, County Monaghan. Home 1939-49.
Below: Four-fifths of Rockcorry. The lady is Lois

scripts were almost verbatim, and they both graduated with first class honours. That was the story. In my class there were two good-looking girls, identical twins, Marie and Victoria Boyd. Remembering the story I arranged for Marie to be placed in the front row in the Whitla Hall and Victoria in the back. When I received their scripts Marie had answered questions 1-5, and Victoria numbers 1, 2, 4, 5 and 6. They differed in the choice of one question, but in 1, 2, 4, 5 their answers could have been written with one copying over the other's shoulder. I enclosed a note to the external examiner saying that they were identical twins and informing him of the seating arrangements. Both were successful, and I received a note of thanks from the examiner to boot.

The same year, 1951, the Board of Education of the General Assembly appointed me to lecture in Religious Education in Stranmillis College. This involved four lectures each week. Not that it was admitted, the reason why I was appointed was that the person I replaced had virtually been driven out. I was to restore order. At first, I had two classes of girls, and one class of boys twice a week. After dealing with the problem of knitting instead of taking notes or joining in discussion had been solved in a manner that alarmed the knitters about how many stitches had been dropped the girls caused no great anxieties. The boys were a different matter. The first day, they just sounded me out. I think by the end of the class they realised I was aware of this. The second day at starting time there were only seven present. I marked the roll as I was required to do, as it had to be returned to the Ministry, and started. Ten minutes later, the door opened and some forty entered. The class continued, but when the bell rang I was reminded that I hadn't called the roll. On being informed that this had been done prior to their coming in, the second round ended. During the third lecture, I stopped and looked at them and said: "I want to point out one thing to you. Rest assured I will not go to the Principal and report you. Whatever happens will be a matter between you and myself as friends in this classroom. There will be no outside help called in. It's between you and me".

From that I never had a minute's disorder and at the end of term they had a golf competition and invited me to take part. I didn't win the prize but we had great fun. I often wonder where they are now. It is necessary to emphasise here how much the years in Stranmillis

(1951-65) meant to me. I probably learned more than the students. In the first two years I lectured on Biblical text and history as did my fellow-chaplains. After that, I took the curriculum and lectured on the various sections in it, showing how a particular passage should be taught to P2, what different emphasis is possible if the same passage is being taught to P6, or why a passage should not be taught until pupils are teenagers. I read Goldman, M'Neill (Drumbo), Hubery, Reuel Howe, Ruedi Weber and others. The classes of boys and girls in Stranmillis sure helped to determine who and what I am.

But, pleasant though these experiences were as a foretaste of a future and different life, the great majority of my time was taken up with equal enjoyment by my church and at Cooke. My early months there had required me to take stands on various issues. One was over the use of the Creed in the Service of Holy Communion. I believe that the faithful should declare their common faith before communicating. I knew that if I said, 'Let us say together the Nicene Creed' there would be difficulty. So I asked the organist, Mr M'Clelland, to practise with the choir Merbecke's setting in the RCH. I announced this as Hymn 725, and many of the congregation joined in.

On the Saturday before the next Communion, I was standing at the bus stop opposite Ralph's shop, when along came a member. In conversation he remarked that to-morrow was communion and asked: "Are we going to have yon creed thing we had at the last communion?"

I asked what he meant.

"Yon creed thing the choir sang".

"Oh", I said, 'you mean Hymn 725".

"Yes", he said, "You know I don't believe a word of it".

"What do you not believe?"

"I don't believe in one baptism for the remission of sins".

I took a New Testament out of my pocket and read Acts ii.38, Repent and be baptized every one of you in the name of Jesus Christ for the remission of sins.

"Now", I said, "do you want me to cut it out of the New Testament also".

"I didn't know it was there", he replied.

The Nicene Creed, then, continued to be part of the service. Here,

I must confess that if I was doing this today I would use a baptismal creed like the Apostles' Creed, not a conciliar like the Nicene. My reason is that the former is the faith into which we are baptised and that we have a unity in baptism, whereas the latter was compiled as a test of orthodoxy. Worship is not for exclusion, and I rejoice that the present minister, Rev. S.J. Campbell, uses the Apostles' Creed — the faith of one's baptism.

Another situation where it was necessary to take a stand involved refusing to let the Orange Society dictate who should preach in Cooke Church.

I was told that a Mr. N— from Sunnyside Street had called to see me. He introduced himself and said that he had come to ask for the use of Cooke Church for an Orange Service. I told him that it was not in my power to grant this and asked if they had ever had it before to be told that they went to Newtownbreda, St.Jude's and Cooke year about, and this year (1949) it was Cooke's turn. I said that as it had been a custom I saw no difficulty, but that I would have to ask the Session's approval.

"Whenever you decide whom you would like to preach tell me and if I approve I will invite him".

"We want Mr Paisley".

"Oh well", I said, "You can have any minister in the Presbyterian Church but you are not having Mr Paisley".

"Then", he said, "we will have to go to Newtownbreda", and left.

Mr. Megaw (Newtownbreda) was well known to me for many years as he had been minister to my father's people in Trinity, Ahoghill. I do not know what he said to Mr Megaw but about an hour and a half later, following a ring at the door, I was surprised to find Mr N—. was there to tell me that he had come to let me know that they were going to Newtownbreda, but that Mr Megaw would not let them through the door unless I was the preacher.

Having to stand in this way for what I believed to be right in worship and in public relations helped to determine who and what I am. An important element in all this was the almost unanimous support I received from the office-bearers and members of the congregation.

At the beginning, I got a strange feeling of unease at Cooke. It was not a family. While many of the people knew each other, it was lacking in depth, and this was true of several groups, none of which was very closely bound to another. I may have been mistaken in this, but I came to the conclusion that many of the members did not know each other because, for twenty years, there had not been any events geared to enabling them to meet and chat to each other. There had been meetings of various kinds, but all only involved going along, sitting in a seat without moving from it, and going home. What I felt was needed was some way to enable the people to mix with each other socially, not simply to come and listen.

In an attempt to deal with the problem, the 'ladies of the congregation' agreed to run 'a daffodil tea'. It was a great success, the tea was good, the people moved from table to table, and up and down the hall, and people living in the same street discovered they belonged to the same church. The ice was broken, and the development of a family relationship went from strength to strength. Cooke was becoming a family of God's people, rejoicing with each other and sharing one another's troubles. It had one spirit and was united. In my opinion, Cooke eventually became a family. My successor, Rev. R.K. Greer, was a friend of many year's standing and perhaps his invitation to me to be Santa Claus at the Christmas party for the children of the primary Sunday School for several years following his installation bears witness to the family spirit. I knew all the children.

"Will you be at home in Candahar Street or at your grannie's in Culdaff for Christmas? Then I'll call there".

"You have two white china dogs on the kitchen mantelpiece. Set them a bit to the side in case I'd knock them over when coming down the chimney".

It was wonderful.

At the same time Cooke did raise certain problems for myself as it was hard going. While each week I still read the Biblical text on which I was preaching in the original, and bought my monthly book, my reading was falling far behind. I found also I needed to be ten-and-a-half stone in September, if I was to turn the scales at nine-and-a-half stone in May.

One was never off duty in Cooke. Miss Janet Wood, the deaconess, was brilliant with children and each year on Youth Sunday conducted a service for young children, for many of whom it was their first church attendance. There was a very good home in Ailesbury Road and this year the mother brought her young son, Stuart, aged about three, to church for the first time. The following Sunday as I was going into church Mrs Young said with a twinkle in her eye:

"I don't know whether I am speaking to you or not".

"What have I done?", I said.

"You don't know the bother you gave me last week".

All this time she was quite obviously enjoying my puzzlement. It turned out that the parents had taught Stuart to kneel beside his bed and place his hands together, like 'the praying hands', when saying his prayers. The previous Sunday in defiance of custom when he knelt down instead of placing his hands together he placed his left elbow on the bed, cupped his hand, and stuck his chin in it. When called on to be a good boy, he said:

"Mammy, that's not the way you pray. This is the way you pray."

"Come on now, be a good boy".

"But, Mammy, this is the way you pray".

"Son, what makes you say that?"

"Well, Mammy, Dr. Barkley was behind us in church today and this is the way he prayed".

In a congregation the size of Cooke, one was never off duty.

6 A broader horizon

At the beginning of 1947, I was simply John Barkley, Presbyterian minister of Second Ballybay and Rockcorry — a person of no great distinction. Within a year, however, I had been appointed to represent the Presbyterian Church in Ireland at the sixteenth General Council of the World Presbyterian Alliance in Geneva, appointed convener for Sabbath Schools, become a member of the Education Board of the Assembly and convener for Grammar School Education in 1948, and made a member of the Assembly's Government Committee in 1947 with special interest in Éire. Further, I was elected Moderator of the Synod of Armagh and Monaghan in 1946. I sought none of these appointments and, apart from the last, when they came they were all a complete surprise.

As well as being a country pastor, I now became a minister with a responsibility at Assembly level. Looking back, I cannot but feel that just as the years 1940-50 were years of academic growth and development, my work in the World Presbyterian Alliance and in Irish Inter-Church relations made the 1950s a period of equal enrichment. This involvement moulded my entire ecclesiastical and theological outlook. The provincial or local had to be transcended by the universal or catholic.

To be going to Geneva in itself was thrilling, not just because of Calvin. This was my first trip overseas. The Irish delegation went by boat and train to Paris, had a meal off some beast tough enough to have been born in the garden of Eden, and took the train from the *Gare du Nord* for Geneva, where we stayed with the Scots in the *Bon Secour* Hotel. (In those days anyone going abroad to represent the General Assembly simply received a return ticket. Needless to say I approve highly of the present practice.) This had the great advantage that in the evening, we could chat together about the events of the day.

This meeting of Council was one of — if not the — most important in the whole history of the Alliance. It was the first after World War Two and, after years of separation, there was a great need to reorganise and strengthen the Alliance. Tentative attempts had been made to renew contacts following the war, but this was the crunch.

I was a new-comer and in many ways a stranger. I did not know a single person except by hearsay, apart from the Irish. Consequently I was surprised on arrival to find myself listed for two study groups — Church Order and Public Worship in the Reformed Churches. I selected the latter under Professor Jean de Saussure (Lausanne) and acted as recording secretary of the group part of the time. In plenary session, the delegates heard all the major papers and then went into study groups. The work load was very heavy so there was little time for relaxation or sightseeing.

Bob Craig (West Church), who had been in College with my father, was the humourist of the party. His best effort came on the platform of Visp railway station. We were waiting for the Milan express to go through and were told it would slow down to about ninety mph. It was a great sight. A lady of the company regularly showed off her French or German so she spoke to a porter, but quite obviously was unable to understand his reply. When someone asked "What did he say?", Bob immediately replied:

"He says he doesn't know Belfast but he's often been to Ballymena".

In Geneva, we discussed, 'Historical Confessions and the Present Witness of the Church'; 'Freedom and Justice in the Light of the Bible'; 'Public Worship in the Reformed Churches'; 'Essentials and Non-essentials in Church-Order'; and 'Presbyterians and the Ecumenical Situation'.

These papers and discussions moulded my whole being and

thinking on many issues — credal confessions, freedom, justice, church-order, worship and ecumenism — so, though at times they will perhaps be a little abstract, some small notice must be taken of them here.

The talks influenced my view on historic confessions in many ways, particularly in critically examining the Documents of Vatican II, supporting the necessity for Declaratory Articles and rejecting fundamentalism.

I also feel that anything like a universal Confession imposed on all congregations or Churches is alien to the genius of the Reformed Church. Although concerned about unity and ecumenical relations the Reformed Churches believed in the variety and diversity of Reformed confessions, recognising them as human products born of specific situations, seeing them as giving a vital consensus, not uniformity. This testified to the kind of ordered freedom sought by the blackmouths.

Linked to this familiar (to me) sense of freedom is justice. This must go beyond simple legalism. In the light of the Cross it must include love, sacrifice and redemption. The group discussing freedom and justice stressed the need for Christian individuals and the Church to be ever critical of the order of society, not in continual condemnation but in prayerful thanksgiving for all that is good, and in humble protest against what is evil. We should beware as Christians of criticising our brother Christians of other lands whose circumstances we cannot possibly fully understand. A Christian individual and Church must always protest against and say NO to any power which disregards the human rights to freedom and responsibility of action.

Here again I have been much influenced in assessing discrimination and rejecting sectarianism and racism. I have consistently refused to condemn the Churches in Russia and call them Communist traitors. Knowing little about South Africa by experience I, while condemning apartheid unequivocally, oppose the Alliance excluding from membership some of the Churches there. There is no such thing as solution by separatism. Here the approach to justice and order, to social questions and goodwill, shows there is no harmony without justice. This statement has its basis in Scripture and in the blackmouth emphasis on human rights.

The group on Public Worship drew up a number of theses:

I. In liturgy, as in doctrine, the Reformed Church recognises as normative... as absolutely binding... only what is revealed by the word of God contained in the Bible (*scriptura sola*).

II. the Reformed Church cannot recognise tradition as a second normative authority alongside the Bible. Therefore she admits variety of liturgical forms in everything that is not fixed by scripture.

III. the Reformed Church respects Tradition as a consultative authority...

IV. historical accidents... having deformed the Reformed liturgy, the necessity for its restoration is recognised everywhere today in the Presbyterian world.

V. This restoration should not consist in 'enrichments' dictated by psychological motives... but... in a purification in line with the original intention of the Reformers, and... in a recovery of evangelical elements found in other traditions and accidentally lost by ours.

VI. A restoration... will... ensure that the character of our liturgy will be both the most purely Reformed and most widely ecumenical.

These theses reminded me of the dissenters' stress on the necessity for purity of worship and Macdonald's words that the organisation of the early Christians "was, first and foremost, an organisation for Worship. Organisation for other purposes might grow out of their Worship, or might lean on it, but was in no case primary". This thinking was deepened at the Emden meeting in 1956 and governed my work in editing *The Book of Public Worship* in 1965.

With the foundation of a World Council of Churches and in the resolutions on church-order, I found what may be described as constitutional guidelines for presbyterianism. Structure is for the service of the Gospel. It must never become a fetter preventing renewal and effectiveness. The law of the church must be based on her doctrine, but canon law should never be given the force of theology.

I find it interesting that inter-church discussions on the subject of Ministry can proceed very cordially until an attempt is made to structure this into Church-Order. Daggers are then immediately drawn.

In I Clement, the doctrine stated is principally one of the continuity and lawfulness of constituted authority. This is not 'episcopal succession from the apostles' as the doctrine is held today by upholders of the 'historic episcopate', that bishops are in origin a distinct order from the presbyterate, and that they alone have succeeded to the place of the Apostles and have inherited the power to ordain. Not even when episcopal lists began to be drawn up in the Apostolic Churches to refute gnosticism, in the last two decades of the second century, had such a doctrine dawned on the Church Fathers. Indeed, if Clement's theory was to be of any value as an apostolic theory of succession, something had to be added in the spheres of doctrine and of discipline. Irenaeus (c.185) supplied the former when he said bishops had also a *certem veritatis charisma,* that is, the gift of discerning and adhering to sound doctrine, a "special endowment enabling them without fail to discern the truth". To put it mildly, history does not show this to be self-evident. In the sphere of discipline, Cyprian (c. 251) claims what Irenaeus had claimed in the sphere of doctrine. Without opposing a constitutional episcopacy, it is well to remember that while some see in bishops a symbol of unity others see in them symbols of persecution and intolerance. Presbyterianism allows considerable liberty of opinion. It is when such a doctrine is held to be normative, or *de fide,* that the point of break-down has to be faced.

The whole question of what role the church should play in the modern world was raised effectively for me by the group on the Church's Mission. It sought how to:

best minister to all the needs of men, in the work of evangelism, teaching, and healing, in social service and in removal of all causes of war, racial prejudice and industrial bitterness and everything that hinders the coming of the Kingdom of God...

In this I welcomed the rejection of the medieval concept of spirituality as an 'escape from the world' as set out by Thomas à Kempis and acceptance of the world as the 'arena of spirituality' as set out by Calvin — and by the dissenters and blackmouths.

The findings of all these groups point to the ethos of presbyterianism being evangelical and ecumenical. Having been a participant in the discussions, they made a big impact on who and what I was to become as a Christian, Catholic and Reformed.

Much of what these reports contain arose out of the horrors of World War Two and a hope that the like could never happen again. The separation and hatred, the distrust and suspicion must be overcome. The transition from world confessional bodies in separation to a World Council of Churches in unity was a witness to the nations. The Council, while at times acting with great caution (it received reports from minority Churches behind closed doors), was definitely dominated by hope.

Perhaps nowhere was the brotherhood of hope more evident than in the daily worship, particularly the Lord's Day Service in the Cathedral Church of St. Pierre and the simple, reverent Thanksgiving afterwards in front of the Monument of the Reformation. There was a deep sense of oneness in the orderliness and dignity of the Reformed rite. There was the centrality of Scripture and the Lord's Supper. There was devotional sincerity and simplicity. There was fellowship and reality.

One thing in particular filled me with delight. Here was World presbyterianism standing for the very things for which the Presbyterian Church in Ireland stood. Here I was a presbyterian within presbyterianism and I saw my Church committed and involved completely.

What a contrast with the present day. As I look at the recent withdrawal of the Presbyterian Church in Ireland from membership of the WCC and the reconstituted British Council of Churches, and the threats of *further* separation, the General Assembly appears to me to have departed from the ecclesiology of the New Testament.

Of course, I also saw the sights. I partook of the body and blood of Christ in St. Pierre. I worshipped in the Church of Marie la Neuve and thought of the Scottish and English exiles. I visited the Academy, now a school, and thought about Calvin, Beza, and the epigones. I went to the Monument of Expiation to Servetus, believing that it was right that it existed even though Servetus was not tried by the law of the Church but by that of the Holy Roman Empire. I visited the Reformation Monument several times and the Headquarters of the Red Cross. I saw the house where Calvin lived, and walked on the lawn where he played bowls reputedly on Sunday afternoons, and took a whole day trip up Lake Leman. It was very peaceful and the mountains were majestic.

I made lifelong friends in Europe, America, Australia, and New Zealand: Dr. Alexander King (Edinburgh), who remained up to his death in 1990, one of my closest friends; J.M. Richardson (Bath), with whom I co-operated in preparing a letter to Pope Pius XII; Pasteur Charles Bartholmé (Strasbourg) and Dr. Frantisek Bednar (Czechoslovakia). I was enabled to invite the Rev. Ernesto Ayassot, whose father and mother had both been shot by the Fascists and who himself had been imprisoned nineteen times, and Rev. Mazerski, formerly a Roman Catholic priest in Poland, to come to Ireland and preach in Cooke Centenary Church.

I also made friends with the Rev. R.L. Findlater (Original Secession Church, Glasgow). The Union between the Secession Church and the Church of Scotland was due to take place at the General Assembly of the Auld Kirk. In April or May, however, he contacted me as the re-unification talks were on the verge of breakdown. The problem was that it was held that the Assembly could approve the Union in 1956, but the ministers of the Secession Church could not take their seats until 1957. If this was to be insisted on the negociations would collapse. He wrote to me asking how Ireland dealt with such situations. I replied that our procedure was that a Memorial was presented, and if its prayer was granted the ministers were immediately welcomed and took their seats. This procedure was adopted, and on the day of the Reunion I was invited to the Scottish Assembly by Mr. Findlater and publically thanked.

I was in Europe again in August, 1950 for the meeting of the Eastern Section of the Alliance in Strasbourg. Again it was a delight to be there. I attended the Reformed Church in the *Rue de Bouclier* in which Calvin had preached when evicted from Geneva in 1538-41. On the Sunday, the Eastern Alliance Service was held in the German speaking *L'Église de S. Paul,* standing at the cleft in the river. This is possibly the most magnificent Reformed church I was ever in, with its great wooden cross standing behind the Holy Table and wide-open apse and central aisle. I visited the great Cathedral where, at the Reformation, Diebold Schwarz had conducted the first Reformed Service in the vernacular on 16 February, 1524, in St. John's Chapel, and where Martin Bucer and Capito preached. Here I also thought of the ecstatic purity of Heinrich Suso and the Dominican Johann Tauler and his society known as the "Friends of God". I saw *L'Horloge astronomique,* and the statues of *La Synagogue* with her blindfolded eyes and *L'Église* with hers wide open looking at the Cross.

I visited the *Conseil de L'Europe* to find that I could have heard the speaker much nearer home, for Mr. Eamonn de Valéra was addressing the House. The people were most friendly and hospitable, but one afternoon's dander round showed that there was considerable distress and want. I had noticed several times row upon row of men sitting along the river fishing. I went over to them and, when I asked how they were getting on, I was told, "There's no fish here, but it puts in the time". They were unemployed. There was nothing to do. So every afternoon they came to fish in a river where there were no fish.

The unemployed of the city were not the only ones who had been left feeling somewhat unwanted. The representatives of the Reformed Church in Hungary received visas to come, but when they arrived at the French border they were refused permission to enter France. This was embarrassing for those of us who lived in the so-called democratic West. But we found a way round it — sort of. Arrangements were made for them to stay in Kehl across the Rhine from Strasbourg, and each evening somebody (including myself on a couple of occasions) went across and briefed them on the day's proceedings.

The South African issue dominated our discussions. Some made extreme demands. It was even suggested that certain of the Churches there should be expelled there and then. I argued that Dr. Pradervand should visit these Churches first and report because I believed it was impossible to achieve a just solution by ostracism and separation. One's influence ends when people stop speaking to each other. Cutting off and expelling people only creates a more dangerous situation.

After the Council, I stayed on in Strasbourg an extra week, because I wanted to see and consult the works of Schwarz and Bucer in the *Bibliothèque Nationale*. Academically and devotionally, this has benefitted me all my life.

My Strasbourg trip ended with a never to be forgotten day. After worship we set out for Hunspach by bus. Two *gendarmes* preceded us on motorbikes with sirens blazing. It was like a royal procession as everything cleared off the roads to let us through. When we arrived we were met by the mayor wearing his sash — not an orange one, but "the blue, the white, the red" of my Uncle John. After a welcome the children's choir, one of the most famous in France, sang to us. By this time some of us, after a roll and a cup of black coffee instead of bacon and egg, were beginning to feel peckish so we were glad to be taken to a large hangar-like building nicely decorated with long tables with white cloths laid with spoons, and knives, and forks but not a bite to eat. Then suddenly, there was the sound of trumpets when in marched two girls dressed in Alsatian native costume playing trombones, followed by two carrying tourines, and after some twenty came two boys playing kettle drums followed by two carrying in each hand a bottle of Alsatian wine — Gewurztraminer.

When the meal was over the local pastor, Pastor Fiedel, told us a wonderful story. When the German army were being driven back towards the end of World War Two, they had dug trenches and placed mines under the villages so that when driven out they could blow them up by remote control. Ingelsheim was completely destroyed this way. How then did we come to be able to visit Hunspach? One Sunday, Pastor Fiedel asked his congregation to pray for him. Everybody knew why. He was going to slip out of the village and beg the German commander to spare the village. No one could help.

One evening at dusk he set out and while he was talking to the German commander suddenly they heard the voices of children singing. The boys and girls of Hunspach had followed their pastor, and there they stood singing the folk songs of Alsace and also some of the psalms they sang in Church. For over half-an-hour, the two men stood in silence and the children sang and sang. Then the commander turned to the pastor and said, "I have learned tonight that I have a greater duty than my duty to my country, I have a duty to humanity. Your village will be spared". So the mines were taken away and a decade later we were able to rejoice with its people.

Hunspach was the nearest thing to heaven I ever was in. Everyone — from the mayor to the grocer, from the teacher to the dustman — was a presbyterian! Who could ever forget such a place! It was a magical day.

In 1953 the Eastern section of the Alliance met at Woudschoten near Utrecht. Two of the main problems facing the Alliance at that time were the persecution of the Waldenses by the Italian government and the murderous persecution of the Reformed church in Columbia. The theme was 'The Word of God in the world of today'. The papers were read in plenary session and studied in groups. I remember one in particular by Professor van Ruler on the interpretation of

Scripture. When he finished the Dutch and Germans jumped up and slapped him on the back. He had done a mighty work, but in my view he had perhaps missed the point, for he had set out a scheme of theology, and then interpreted the Scriptures in the light of it. I had always admired Utrecht for how it faced up to the lectures in Karl Barth's *Credo* in 1935-36, but this lecture seemed to me to fall into the same "miry clay".

One afternoon in Utrecht, I visited the statue of S. Willibrord, who with all due respects was not educated at Mellifont. I also visited the University and the *Grosskirche*. In the latter, there is an interesting Evangelists' Window. They had no haloes and it set me thinking about what the evangelists and apostles were like as men when stripped of all the sentimental ideas with which we surround them. They were an interesting if, at times, a rum group.

We went to public worship on the Sunday at Emmeloord in the N.E. Polder. There we had an experience I have never had before or since. After sermon, the Pastor announced three offerings with two retiring offerings. I had not prepared myself with small change and so felt 'we was robbed'. Afterwards I discovered that the Dutch were like the Irish presbyterians of a former generation who put a penny on the plate and were satisfied.

In 1953, the General Assembly nominated me to be a delegate to the seventeenth General Council of the Alliance in 1954. During the autumn I was surprised to be informed, "You can only be sent to Princeton if you are prepared to pay half your fare". I said I couldn't afford to do so. So a substitution was made. I missed a stimulating session. The Council appointed a commission "to formulate afresh the Reformed doctrine of Ordination, and of the service in the Church of minister, elder, and deacon, with particular reference to the ministry of women". Though not present, I was appointed Convener and presented the Commission's Interim-Report at the eighteenth General Council at Sao Paulo, Brazil, in 1959.

The issues which had interested me at Princeton and Evanston were the persecution of the Reformed Church in Columbia and government discrimination against the Reformed Church in Greece. The former had been raised in the Irish General Assembly in 1954. They had written to the Most Rev. Gerald P. O'Hara, Papal Nuncio, and His Eminence John Cardinal D'Alton. The Nuncio replied that the "authentic and thoroughly trustworthy information, gathered from both the ecclesiastical and civil authorities, differs radically from that contained in your letter", but agreed to receive a delegation. The Princeton report states:

three-fourths of the country are closed to Protestant Christian witness... they are refused the right of assembly... The revival of the spirit of the Inquisition in Columbia has confined the Evangelical Church to a ghetto existence.

The Council expressed to the Synod of the Presbyterian Church in Columbia, "their deep concern, sympathy, and solidarity" and requested the WCC publicly to protest against this flagrant infringement of religious liberty. Its stand was worthy of the blackmouths.

As chairman of the British Churches Committee at that time I had a special interest in the situation, as along with the Rev. J.M. Richardson (Bath) I had been appointed to address a letter to Pope Pius XII on the matter. Here we made an interesting discovery — that it was not possible to bring it to his notice unless it was handed in by an accredited ambassador to the Holy See. Franco was no use, neither was de Gaulle, so we had to use the British Foreign Office. They refused to handle it. It was rewritten and again we were politely refused. So it was rewritten again and the Foreign Office agreed to act, in my opinion reluctantly. The writing and re-writing, and ensuring full documentation took time. Meanwhile the persecution continued, the burning of the Reformed Church in Palmira on 13 December 1955 bringing the total to forty-six churches razed in seven years.

In fairness, it must be said that the Pope did intervene eventually but with what, in my opinion, was only limited success. On the other hand, perhaps it was all he could do. Who and what I am was certainly influenced by these events.

The other issue at Princeton in which I had a special interest concerned my friend George Hadjiantoniou, Moderator of the Evangelical Church of Greece and minister of Second Athens. His Church had been damaged and obstacles had been placed in the way of its restoration. Here the Alliance held to the principle of the right to dissent and justice for minorities. There was some tension in raising this at the Evanston Assembly of the WCC, but the strength of the Reformed presence ensured it was. Indeed, the WCC had considerable success in freeing the Evangelical Greek Church from disabilities. This incident has a salutary lesson for Irish Presbyterianism. Had presbyterianism withdrawn from the WCC in sympathy with the Greek Evangelical Church instead of continuing to be a member, there was a distinct possibility that in the circumstances of the period no public action would have been taken. One has no influence when one is absent.

Irish presbyterianism is no longer a member of the WCC or the newly structured Council of Churches for Britain and Ireland but it is nice to remember that once upon a time, though harassed by fundamentalism, Irish presbyters did help the small Reformed Church of Greece.

The British Churches' Committee of the WARC in 1956 rejoiced in the fact that for the first time the Executive Committee had met in a People's Republic in Prague. As well as Czechoslovak pastors, representatives of the Reformed Churches in Romania and Poland were able to be present. This meeting culminated in a great act of thanksgiving and worship in the Bethlehem Chapel, the pulpit of John Hus and the cradle of the Hussite Reformation. The year began with signs of an easing of the international tension between East and West. Sadly, it ended with revolution and suppression in Hungary. Relations between the Alliance and the great Reformed Church in Hungary have always been close. So has the relationship between Hungary and Irish presbyterianism, and within a month of the suppression over £25,000 had been raised for relief. Refugees were taken into Irish Universities. One, Istvan Kardos, became a student in the Presbyterian College.

He had escaped with his wife and their first child was born in a refugee camp. On completing his course, he was ordained by the Presbytery of Belfast and appointed to work among Hungarian refugees in Britain under the auspices of the British Council of Churches. Later, feeling that he owed something to Irish presbyterianism, he returned to Ireland and was installed in Minterburn and Caledon. He served our Church faithfully until he was forced to leave. He was an excellent scholar and a person of great integrity. As he had been an Olympic horseman, one of the duties of Professor Boyd, as warden, was to supply him with a horse once or twice a week. His young family, all of primary school age, were abused by some Protestants who forgot their loyalty to the Gospel and instead followed the tenets of Irish party politics.

Our idea had been to try and integrate the refugees in Britain into the community but this proved to be an impossibility, particularly with the elderly and those who knew no English. Also there was a strong desire that their Hungarian culture and customs should not be completely lost, so a house was bought at St. Dunstan's Road, London, and turned into a worship and community centre. I am proud to have had the honour of presiding at its dedication.

As well as caring for refugees, we organised contributions and assistance for the rebuilding of the Reformed Church in Hungary itself. This was vital for the future of Christ's kingdom in Hungary, and I again thank the men of Cooke Centenary's indoor bowling club for their generosity.

In 1964 the European area of the Alliance had to reaffirm its insistence on the obligation of majority Churches — Roman Catholic and Orthodox in particular — to uphold the principle of religious liberty for minority churches. We also had to set up a committee to minister to Roman Catholic priests who had left the Church of Rome. The principle of the Alliance was:

We never encourage any priest to leave his Church, but when they come to us after having made a responsible decision on their own, we have an obligation to help them to rehabilitate themselves in an active Christian life.

Some continued academic theological studies, some became advisers to the Reformed Church, some became Reformed pastors, some became farmers or businessmen, and some retained a connection with the Church of Rome. All received understanding.

The eighteenth General Council of the Alliance was held in Sao Paulo in July-August, 1959, on the theme 'The Servant Lord and His Servant people'. Our meetings were held in a great stark white igloo of a modernistic building — the sort of thing one expects to see in *Dr Who* — in the Ibirapelra Park and we had our meals in the Museum of Modern Art.

Of its five reports, I wish only to refer to the one on the Service of the State. I mention it particularly because it seems to me to be where all the Churches in Ireland, without exception, have failed.

The Report says to the Churches:

1. Your primary task is to honour God and to win men to Jesus Christ and teach them to serve the Lord. From this it follows that your most important service to the State is to raise up citizens of unselfish loyalty and intelligent commitment to the common good who are the greatest need of every State.
2. You should teach and encourage your members to hear and heed the clear call of Christ to social and political service, remembering that the Lord Jesus Christ is served in such places as social clubs, directors' board rooms, trade union halls, market places, universities and legislatures as well as under the church's roof.
3. Your primary relationship as a Church to those of your membership who become officials or authorities in the State is pastoral service to them. You should pray for them, encourage them to see their work as under God, and surround them with Christian love, not forgetting other leaders of the State that are outside your fellowship.
4. As a Church you have a duty to speak to the State in behalf of justice, freedom, and mercy for all men of every race and station.
5. As a Church you have a duty to listen to the Word of God and on the basis of your spiritual insight to speak to the issues of economics and politics.
6. You have also the duty to pray for all those who because of sincere Christian conscience resist the State and are in danger.
7. Let your political interest and activity be centered on those issues and cases which help establish the civil conditions of responsible freedom for men to serve their sovereign God.

The report then warned:

1. Never confuse or identify the Church with any established regime or revolutionary party...
2. Never confuse or allow to be confused your Church's doctrine or order with ideologies such as capitalism, communism or socialism...
3. Never use the power, influence, or prestige of your Church... to win from the State benefits for your own Church which would damage the interests of others...
4. Never seek to use the power of the State to enforce upon any man, against his will or conscience, your Church's interests, ends, or programs.

These guidelines and warnings are worthy of blackmouth principles. But the report also appears to me to depict the failure of the Irish Churches. We all need to hear and heed these warnings.

At a plenary session on Friday, 31 July, I presented the Commission's 'Interim Report on Ordination'. The discussion continued on the Monday, when the following resolution was adopted:

The Eighteenth General Council expresses its deep appreciation to the Commission on Ordination and the Ministry, headed by Professor Barkley, and its thanks to its distinguished chairman and members for the Interim Report hereby received.

Ordination is an act of God within His Church. Its essence is prayer with the laying on of hands. It is not necessary here to set out the contents of the Report except perhaps, as some dispute it in Irish presbyterianism today, to say that the Commission held "that in principle it sees no reason why the ministry of women should be considered as a special category", that "this question cannot be solved simply on an analogy with, or as a response to, the changing position of women in modern secular life", it "can never be considered as a matter of 'rights'... it is a task to which one is called, not a right which one claims", that "just as Jesus did not ignore the society in which he lived... the Church cannot do so", "that there is no question of giving a place in Church life to the separate contributions of men and women", and that:

there are no theological obstacles to the full participation of men and women in all orders of the ordained ministry of the church. More than this, the majority of the Commission is convinced that there are sound theological arguments in favour of the full sharing of the ministry by men and women.

In the Presbyterian Church in Ireland women have been received, on the same conditions as men, in the eldership since 1926, and in the Ministry of Word and Sacrament since 1973. Though the Judicial Commission did not consider the latter involved a constitutional change, it was referred under the Barrier Act to Presbyteries, and the Doctrine Committee was directed to draw up a report on 'The Ordination of Women' before they voted. Eighteen Presbyteries voted giving approval with three against, by 410 votes to 132. It was then enacted in the General Assembly with no dissents recorded.

As a result of the discussion on the Report, I was nominated from the floor for the chairmanship of the Department of Theology of the World Presbyterian Alliance. This was a surprise. As was what followed, for the committee making the appointment was somehow informed that the Irish church would not pay my expenses if I was appointed. I am not saying that I was sabotaged, but how this came to be known to the committee, I don't know. In the end, however, a certain amount of common-sense prevailed, for my life-long friend from Geneva days, Professor James I. McCord, got the job.

In 1959 the Irish representatives to the WPA conference in Brazil were Lady MacDermott, Mrs. Suzanne Wilton, Rev. J.S.P. Black and myself. Stewart, a classmate of mine in College and a good companion, and I decided to go by sea. So off we went from Tilbury on the *S.S.Argentina Star*. It was lovely sailing up the Tagus in the morning light and seeing the *Monumento a Christo Roi* watching over the city of Lisbon. We hired a taxi and went down to Estoril, proceeded to the white marble Stadium of Light, the home of Benfica, and quite a change from the Brandywell and Solitude, and walked the beautiful cloisters of *Mosteiro dos Jeronimos*.

Next stop was Tenerife. Here we went to the top of the volcano, and it being Sunday worshipped in the Candelaria Sanctuary. Some passengers threw coins into the clear deep blue water and the boys dived for them. The first port of call in Brazil was Bahia. Stewart wanted to shop so I wandered round on my own. I saw a cock-fight. I saw poverty the like of which I had never seen before. I saw the *Igreija de S. Francisco* — a Church completely decorated with gold leaf. Today, many would say why not sell it and relieve the poverty of the city. On the other hand, when it was built Brazil was a major gold exporter and the Church was so decorated because it was held that only the best is good enough to furnish God's house. In its setting of squalor it made one think.

There was a brief call at Rio de Janeiro. We saw the harsh desolation of prison island, in contrast to the magnificence of the approach to the city. Then it was on to Santos where we disembarked. This was an experience. A porter carried your bag to the deck. If you took it yourself no-one would touch it. Another took it to the quayside and set it down. He had to be tipped. Another took it to outside the customs. He too had to be tipped. Another carried it inside. He had to be tipped. The bag was all but taken asunder and the customs man gave it to another porter. He took it to the path outside. When tipped, he rushed off, I assume to look for another victim. The racket is so well developed and successful they do not need a trade union.

The work load was so heavy, free-time was very limited. Several evenings there were entertainments which introduced us to Brazilian music and culture. We saw the Rio Carnival. We visited a snake farm. We worshipped in the *Catedral Evangelica de Sao Paulo.*

The Alliance Council coincided with the centenary of presbyterianism in Brazil. Our meetings ended on Friday and we were to go by bus to Rio the next day for the centenary, when at the evening meal there was an announcement: "Would Professor Barkley speak to Dr. Moares at the close of this meal. It is urgent". I had known Dr. Benjamin Moares for years. I wondered what he wanted. However, when I saw him I soon learned.

"John, you are to deliver a lecture on Presbyterianism in Britain at the Press Centre at 2 o'clock on Monday in Rio de Janeiro. There is a Congresso Mundial de Historia do Presbyterianismo." This was the first I knew of it.

I hadn't a book. In Rio, the centenary celebrations began with a Service in the *Catedral Presbyteriana,* followed by an Evangelical concert in *Estadio Gilberto Cardoso,* where a choir of about two hundred sang the Hallelujah Chorus. I bought a record of this, little knowing the trouble it would cause with the customs in London — they were certain it contained some subversive coded message.

The celebrations were to continue with the opening of the General Assembly on Monday morning. I took Monday morning off to prepare my lecture and went along for lunch to find the members of Assembly sunning themselves on the steps. I asked how the meeting had gone to be informed that it hadn't started as the Moderator had not yet arrived. I arrived at the Press Centre about one o'clock. Two o'clock came, so did 2.30 about which time I was informed that they could not begin because the interpreter had gone to Copacabana for a bathe.

We started about four o'clock and ended, after questions, about 5.30. I do not remember the exact content of my lecture, but I do remember two things. The first was that many were tired of having heard over and over again that the Brazilian Church was a daughter of the American, so I began by saying that the Presbyterian Church in Ireland was the grandmother of Brazilian presbyterianism, and the Church of Scotland the great-grandmother. The second thing was that I was extremely lucky to remember that John Calvin had, in the sixteenth century, sent a special mission to Brazil, which sadly had failed because of political intrigue, so I made good play of this.

Before turning from Brazil, reference must be made to President Kubitchek of Brazil's address to the members of the Alliance. He said he spoke as a Christian and a Catholic. He praised the contribution presbyterians had made to life and culture in Brazil, declaring "Our land glories in the complete religious liberty which its citizens enjoy". It was an inspiring experience, for never before in Latin American history had a Chief of State officially attended a Protestant Church gathering. I rejoice in having been present.

The next meeting of the General Council was arranged for Frankfurt in 1964, and that its theme would be 'Come, Creator Spirit'. I was not surprised when I was not nominated to go to Frankfurt for I had had the feeling for several years that this was on the cards, partly because I had opposed the abolition of the British Churches Committee of the Alliance on which some had set their hearts. I was, and still am, of the opinion that this was a mistake. There is now no unifying Reformed voice for these islands. This has seriously undermined its influence in Britain and Ireland.

I know I would have loved to have gone to Frankfurt because of the theme and to see the *Weisfrauenkircke* in which the English exiles worshipped in the sixteenth century. I missed meeting friends, but it was right that I was not a delegate, and I did get to worship in the *Weisfrauenkircke* eventually, when representing the Irish Council of Churches in Germany in 1985.

In 1970, meeting in Nairobi, the World Presbyterian Alliance and the International Congregational Council united to form the World Alliance of Reformed Churches. The term 'reformed' should "always be understood and accepted in the sense of *semper reformanda*" (always being reformed).

Today, the WARC consists of 161 churches with an estimated 74 million members in 82 countries. I am no longer a member of its General Council, but I am still consulted from time to time, and I try to keep in touch. I am grateful for having had the chance to be a full participant in the affairs of the Alliance at an important stage in its evolution. The experience enriched me and I hope I have been able to make a useful contribution in return.

7 Principal Barkley

When Dr. A.F. Scott Pearson, professor of Church History in the
Presbyterian College, Belfast, died in 1952, I applied at the 1953
General Assembly for the vacant Chair. Today, there is a Board of
Nomination, however, in my day the appointment was made by a
vote of the General Assembly, and so the matter intimately concerned
the whole church. This made the task of applying a labour of Hercules,
for one had to draw up an application and post, at one's own expense,
some 1,100 copies to the members of Assembly. There were six
applicants (three Irish, two Scots, and one Australian). In the final
vote, the Rev. W.I. Steele (First Derry) and I each received 375
votes. As the Moderator, Principal J.E. Davey, did not exercise a
casting vote, the result was a tie and it was agreed to call a special
meeting of Assembly in September to make the appointment. But
again it was a tie, Mr. Steele and myself each receiving 362 votes.

This created a delicate situation. It meant that I would have to
face my congregation for another next twelve months knowing that
the whole thing would arise again in a year's time. However, I
received nothing but kindness and understanding in Cooke Centenary
congregation. Then there was the question of what to do if invited to
preach? If I agreed, would I be accused of looking for votes? If I
refused, would I be thought disobliging? I resolved this by deciding
neither to give nor accept invitations, the only exceptions being to
exchange twice with my pal Bill Haslett, in Crumlin Road.

But this was not the end of it. 1953 marked the centenary of the opening of the College, and a number of public and private events were arranged to celebrate the occasion. I do not know who was at the Centenary dinner or any other private festivity, and as I was not invited to these, I did not go to any of those which were public, seeking to avoid misinterpretation or misunderstanding. Neither did I attend the Public Opening or Closing of the Session 1953-54, though I normally did so. My main relaxation, apart from indoor bowls on Thursday evenings, was a trip each Saturday with Bill to Solitude to support the Reds. I think the wisdom of my decision to keep a low profile may be seen in a letter I received from the Moderator-designate, dated 3 February, 1954:

Dear John,
You probably know by this time that I have been nominated as Moderator-designate of the General Assembly for next June. So that you may know the position this is to inform you that if the vote is again a tie between you and Billy Steele I will be giving my casting vote in his favour.
Yours sincerely,
John Knowles.

I replied by return of post:

Dear Johnny,
Thank you for your letter. I know the Assembly is entitled to appoint whomsoever it pleases and that you are free to vote for whoever you like. Wishing you a successful year in office.
Yours faithfully,
John M. Barkley.

John Knowles was a man whom I greatly admired. I knew the letter was not personal. We knew each other sufficiently well for me to say that he knew that I recognised his right to vote as he wished. However, I must admit that I was surprised to receive it.

At the Assembly in 1954, I was appointed by 451 votes to 429. At this point, I was called into the House to sign the Westminster *Confession of Faith* but I could not be found. The students had kidnapped me and taken me for a ride on a horse and dray round the centre of the city. When this was explained to the Moderator, he declared the students to be guilty of contempt and demanded that they apologise for insulting the House. Some of the students appeared and Billy Moran apologised. I felt sad that the Assembly reacted the way it did. However, I duly signed the *Confession of Faith* and thanked the Assembly for appointing me.

These events produced a brief saga. At the Public Opening of the College, the Presbytery of Belfast installed me, and in the Service the Moderator of the General Assembly gave the Charge, but, like many other Charges I have heard, it wasn't a Charge. Rather it was good advice telling me not to be disturbing the peace of the College, to co-operate and not fight with the other professors, and suchlike. Then he turned to his own student days and told how in his time there was one professor who was not on speaking terms with any of his colleagues. This he emphasised several times and quite inconsistently informed us that this professor was the only member of the faculty from whom he had learned any thing. It was all very strange.

Further, at that time the practice was for representatives of the supervising committee to visit the classes of every professor annually. Who should they appoint in my first year to be Visitor to the Church History class, but the Moderator! When this was rumoured in the light of, as they saw it, his recent humiliation of them, the students were mad. Two of them saw me and asked if the rumour was true, and when I said it was, they said: "We'll kill him". I did not take this literally, but said, 'Well if you do, take care not to let me see you doing it'.

The day of Visitation arrived. Everyone — including the professor — was in class at 8.55 a.m., faces glowing with expectancy. We waited, but the Moderator did not appear. Perhaps providentially, his car had broken down in Banbridge.

This annual Visitation appeared to some (including myself) like appointing a professor and then keeping an eye on him. It pointed to a lack of trust. Consequently when revising the bye-laws for Union Theological College, as Visitors in College fulfilled the same function to professors and classes as Presbytery Visitations did to ministers and congregations, the practice was altered on my proposal to "visiting in rotation one department each year" and should it be necessary "the College Management Committee may visit any department at any time, seven day's notice having been given". This protects an inalienable right of the General Assembly without giving the practice the appearance of an inquisition.

The College now became the centre of my world. My pastoral visiting ended. I moved amongst new sets of people. My pattern of reading had to change completely. No longer was it a case of buying a book a month. I had to keep abreast. A new book was published by Trevor Roper, A.J.P. Taylor, Hans Kung, or someone else. It had to be read. Over the summer I set myself a course of reading. It might be the Ante-Nicene Fathers, Documents of Vatican II, a Document of the WARC or of the WCC, and so on. One dare not ignore the latest work by either Rahner and Ratzinger, or Jeremias and Cullmann, or others if giving a paper to a learned Society. To this had to be added exercising a critical openness to source material. I familiarised myself with what was going on in the Scottish universities. Further, I annually checked with St. Patrick's College, Maynooth, as to what books were prescribed there. Many of them were idential with those in ACB. This was not an ecumenical study of history, but it did avoid a completely sectarian approach and ensured that I and my students received a multiplicity of views.

I also found that I was given several hats:

I was a member of Faculty in the Presbyterian College.

I was a member of the Presbyterian Theological Faculty, Ireland.

I was a member (if I had the academic qualifications) of the Faculty of Theology in Queen's University.

I was a member of the Joint-Assembly's/ Edgehill Committee.

In addition I was also an *ex officio* member of the Board of Studies and most of its sub-committees.

Periodically, I also had to fulfil the duties of some administrative office: Librarian, Bursar, Warden, Secretary, Vice-Principal, or Principal. It may seem difficult to believe, but when I was appointed there were absolutely no administrative staff: everything had to be done by the professors.

It is interesting to chart how a situation like this arose. Unlike the Anglicans who had a Divinity School reserved for them in Dublin University, and the Roman Catholics who had Maynooth provided for them, we presbyterians had to build our own Colleges — Belfast in 1853 and Magee, Derry, in 1865, and if a presbyterian wished to graduate in theology, he had to go to Scotland or the Continent. No presbyterian had graduated in theology in an Irish University at the date when I was received as a student for the Ministry in 1929. To deal with this grievance, a Charter was granted to the Presbyterian Theological Faculty, Ireland, in 1881, when Gladstone conferred upon the Faculty of the Presbyterian College, Belfast, together with the three theological professors in Magee College, Derry, the power to grant degrees in Divinity.

During the years 1922-31, when the number of professors in MCD was reduced to one, some disputed the validity of the Charter and no degrees were conferred. Many, including my father, feared that the ACB Faculty were deliberately allowing the Charter to fall into desuetude as an enticement to get a Faculty of Theology in QUB, an option then under discussion. So they took the opinion of Mr. Arthur Black and that of Lord Sands. I remember well the scene when these were read out in the Assembly. W.P. Hall suggested that as they had not awarded any DDs for ten years they should now give four instead of two, whereon Principal Paul jumped up and shouted, "Remember the Assembly have nothing to do with it, only the Faculty". He sure was angry. Eventually everyone agreed that no restrictions would be imposed on the working of the Charter of 1881. At the union of ACB and MCD to form Union Theological College, I ensured the incorporation into the Act of Parliament in 1978 a clause securing its rights under the Charter.

Queen's College had been founded as "a godless college" in 1849, which meant that it had no faculty of theology. Some pressed for the creation of such a faculty. Others were opposed. Eventually the Courts decided that there was nothing to prevent the establishment of such a faculty in QUB "provided that no public funds were used for this purpose". When, in 1926, the University finally decided to take such a step the method adopted was to have 'recognised colleges' with 'recognised teachers'. In 1927, the Presbyterian College became a 'recognised college', as did Edgehill in 1951, the Baptist College in 1977, and St Mary's College in 1966. Now it is quite an ecumenical faculty.

I think I am the only person ever to have been removed from membership of the QUB faculty. I became a member in 1954 and was removed from the roll of members the year I retired when Dr Richard Talbert, lecturer in Ancient History, was Dean. This strange and inexplicable act, which flabbergasted my friends on the faculty, meant I could no longer act as supervisor for higher degrees.

On my arrival the Faculty consisted of Principal J.E. Davey who had been my professor in Old and New Testament, Professor R.J. Wilson who had lectured me in Hebrew language, Professor J.L.M. Haire, who had been a fellow student and whose father had been my professor in Systematic Theology. There was now no professor of Practical Theology, Professor Robert Corkey, who had taught me, having retired, and the work of the chair being given to congregational ministers.

The theory was that they knew the practical problems. This was possibly true, but I have always thought it wasn't much use if they hadn't the academic or experiental knowledge to deal with them. For example, I found it difficult to convince students of the Biblical understanding of the Apostolic Benediction as in the Scottish and Westminster Assembly tradition when the lecturer in Practical Theology rejected Reformed practice.

My old professor, Dr. F.J. Paul, had died suddenly in 1941 and been succeeded by Professor A.F. Scott Pearson, an authority on Elizabethan puritanism. So there remained a strong nucleus from my student days of men whom I held in high respect and with whom I had no desire to fight. Here, let me say that throughout my years as a professor there could not have been a friendlier or more co-operative group. Integrity and friendship were the hallmarks of the faculty. They were also the hallmarks of the relationship between the professors' families and houses.

I found the Church History curriculum unchanged since my student days. We still had the problem of God being treated as if He was dead during the years 1451-1484 and since 1647. My first task was to try and correct this. I had to show that there is no such thing as Church History. There is History and within that history the Church exists and that this means that economics, geography, and social conditions, as well as success and failure, fidelity and deceit have a place. I had learned that, when the Papacy needed money, you had an increase in the sale of Indulgences, that Regensberg is in Bavaria so Luther dare not attend the Diet there in 1541 as the Bavarian princes wanted "War bloody War" and so would have seized him and carried out his murder in accordance with the Edict of Worms. I had to answer the question, was it because Geneva was situated at a crossroads of Europe and Wittenberg was not that Lutheranism was confined chiefly to Germany and Scandinavia whereas Calvinism became an international movement? Or, again, was it because Scotland owed allegiance to the Avignon pope, whereas England owed it to the Roman that the reforming movement in the two countries followed different lines? I knew the 'reforming movement' affected the whole of Europe from Poland and Hungary to Scotland, and from Scandinavia to the Mediterranean. It wasn't limited to protestantism. I knew the education polity of the Jesuits was based on Calvin's Genevan Academy. Astronomy had revolutionised science, the world went round the sun. The centre of the earth had moved from the Tiber to Portugal and Spain, and on to Holland and Britain. I had to show that chronology is not history, that history has a philosophy, and that history is a continuous flowing river. It does not start *de novo* each morning or each New Year's Day. There is continuity. How far I was ever successful in achieving this is for others to say, not me.

It was not always easy to know how I was getting on in lectures because, before coming to College students were often warned "not to believe anything Barkley teaches". Let me say that I owe thanks to the twenty or twenty-five students who, when leaving College came to my study and thanked me for all I had done for them; they had not expected it as they had been given this advice before coming to College. My hope is that I treated every student with the same objectivity as Dr. Oulton treated me.

Also in this context, I must say a special word of thanks to Barkley Wallace (Bushmills). One day in November 1956, I was walking up Botanic Avenue and he was about twenty yards ahead of me. When he came to the traffic lights at University Street they were against him and looking back he saw me and waited. After a few words, out of the blue he said:

"I would like to thank you for your Church History lectures, Sir".

I was a bit surprised because, in class, Barkley watched me impassively and I was never sure whether he was treating what I said with contempt or approval. So I thanked him saying that he was the first student ever to thank me for my lectures and that I would never forget it.

"Well, it's this way. There are lots of things I believe but I didn't know why. Your lectures are giving me the reasons".

My hope is that others benefited in this way also. I remember the incident with deep gratitude for Barkley was completely unaware of my need for recognition and encouragement.

While it is a generalization and does not apply to all students, I think there has been a change in attitude to books since my student days. I cannot think of a fellow-student who would have had a prejudice against an author or who would have refused to read anything written by him. Books were there to be enjoyed, not simply to use to pass examinations. A book might contain something new. If it was rumoured to be 'not sound' that was an additional reason for reading it. To us a book like G.L. Prestige's *Fathers and Heretics* was a gift from above, not something repulsive, something to be afraid of in case we in our righteousness might be contaminated. There is no need to fear the like of Robinson's *Honest to God*. Certainly, I cannot think of anyone who would have shown his orthodoxy by denouncing it in a sermon without having read it. To do so would have been in my student days held by all to be contemptible and dishonest. In the last twenty-five years, there appears to me to have been a great change of attitude on issues like these. One should read to learn not simply to confirm one's prejudices.

Principal Paul used to stress that if one was to be a successful pastor in Ireland it was essential to know Irish history (a remark which applies to many diciplines). But, apart from about four lectures on St. Patrick, he never lectured on the latter. There was no class in Irish history in College when I was appointed a professor, so I approached the Faculty and the Board of Studies with the hope of establishing it as a course to be taken by all students. I was fortunate in that my proposal was welcomed, and also in the fact that at this time whole series of distinguished studies began to be published, works by T.W. Moody, F.X. Martin, J.C. Beckett, J.G. Simms, L. M'Cracken, F.S.L. Lyons, A.T.Q. Stewart, J.A. Murphy and others. It was a time in which to rejoice. I am not sure that some of the students were ever able to see that the real victors at the Battle of the Boyne were the Papacy and the Established Church, not the presbyterians or Roman Catholics of Ireland, or how far the test of human rights leads one to believe in two '98 Rebellions, one in the north based on the Rights of Man and one in the south which contained sectarian elements (or, indeed, that the latter undermined the former); or that there are not two but many traditions in Ireland, or to take an objective view of events and reject 'triumphalist attitudes', etc. To try to answer that question would be conjecture on my part.

However I was very touched at the Public Closing of the College, in 1981, to receive a signed presentation copy of *Challenge and Conflict,* edited by Professor J.L.M. Haire, who wrote in the foreword:

This series of essays on 'Challenge and Conflict' within the Presbyterian Church in Ireland over the past three centuries is being published both to make available the results of much historical research and at the same time to express the gratitude of the other essayists to one of their number, Rev. Principal John M. Barkley, for the very large contribution he has made to our understanding of the history of our Church.

One of the things that pleased me here, was being able to discover the original source of the *logo,* the Burning Bush with *Ardens sed Virens* and its Irish setting amidst shamrocks and thistles, harps and round towers, Irish wolfhounds and the Open Bible. Tragically, the Irish setting is no longer prominent.

In all three areas — Church and Irish history and Symbolics — I enjoyed the lectures, but sometimes I met with disappointment: to find Jesus spelled 'Jeasus'; symbols spelled 'cymbals'; Barkley spelled 'Barclay'; to find some essays copied . One year, I set three essays on the Council of Trent to find (in spite of having put six recent publications into the library) that the most recent work quoted in any of the three was dated 1853. In 1966 or 1967, during the scheme providing Optionals, I studied the texts of Vatican II, prepared 176 pages of notes and offered it as an Optional. Not a single student enrolled for it. Of course, there was no specific reason why anyone should. At the same time, after all my efforts to provide an accurate analysis of the texts and a detailed examination of the views of Roman Catholic and Protestant commentators, I was a bit disappointed.

Kidnapped by hooligans (see chapter seven).   Below:
Cooke Centenary, Belfast: Presbyterian Church or glorified sectarian hall?

A view from the edge: the committee on Worship in session at the World Presbyterian Alliance, Geneva, 1948. From left: myself, Dr. R. Thomas (Austria); Prof. F. Bednar (Czechoslovakia); Prof. W. Niesel (Germany); Prof. J.I. McCord (America); Prof. J. de Sassure (Switzerland); Pastor R. Mobbs (Switzerland); Dr. H. Eberard (France). Below: My Friend Bill. The Rev. W.L. Hazlett, who died tragically after a long illness in 1960.

Presenting the report on Ordination to the World Presbyterian Alliance, Rio.
I hope you like the halo. Below: Union Theological College, Belfast, commonly
known as Assembly's College — home of erudition.

Rio 1959, at the celebrations to mark the centenary of presbyterianism in Brazil. Mrs. Nady Werner, receiving the Scottish and Irish delegations: A.R. Shillinglaw, myself, R. Stuart Louden, J.S.P. Black.   Below: Agnes' Cake. A tribute to services rendered. On the left my ecclesiastical journeying rendered in icing, on the right Cliftonville beating Linfield. Up the Reds!

Prior to 1954, only two former students of the College had graduated Doctor of Philosophy in the Faculty of Theology in Queen's University. After I had been at the College for a short time, a considerable number enrolled for higher degrees in the University Faculty. Further, with the B.D. becoming a primary degree it became possible to do honours. In 1972, R.S. Tosh (BBC) gained first class honours as did D.R. Purce (Loughbrickland and Scarva) in 1977, and four others obtained Two-Ones. I owe a great deal to the research and honours students. Their creativity prevented me ever coming to treat my work as simply routine. From them I learned a lot.

The same is true, in a different way, of my lectures to various learned Societies. The first was in 1960, when I was invited to give a paper at the Annual Conference of the Society for the Study of Theology in Gonville and Caius College, Cambridge. Over the years invitations followed from Geneva, Germany, Scotland, England, America and the Republic; and the subjects varied between Church History, Irish History and Liturgiology. While it is for others, rather than myself, to assess the erudition of these, I did work hard to ensure that I upheld the good name and academic standing of the College.

During the early sixties in theological circles, there was a great deal of discussion about inter-disciplinary co-operation. The session 1966-67 was epoch making. It was decided to organise a course in which all members of Faculty would participate. The subject chosen was Baptism. Forty lectures were to be prepared by the staff, and owing to the different interpretations by the various Churches, it was agreed to invite an Anglican, a Baptist, a Roman Catholic, and a member of the Society of Friends to give one lecture each.

Because a Roman Catholic was invited to give one lecture out of a total of forty-four, the action of the Faculty was raised in the Assembly. In the discussion, after an unholy spate of distortion and misrepresentation, and it was proposed "That... the General Assembly disapprove of the visit of Father Hurley to address students in Assembly's College". However an amendment was moved approving the action of the Faculty, "that our students may have a fuller appreciation of what each interpretation of the doctrine of Baptism means to the members of that particular branch of the Church". The amendment was carried by 217 votes to 118, an addendum being added that the Doctrine Committee examine the doctrinal problems involved. An 'elder of the Presbyterian Church' in a letter to *The Belfast Telegraph* summed up the position accurately when he wrote:

There can be only two reasons for being unwilling to hear what another party has to say... Either you believe you have nothing to learn; or you fear you cannot defend your cause.

The 118 showed that they had never seen Calvin's *Acta Synodi Tridentinae cum Antidoto,* let alone read and studied it. It is a full reprint of the text of the decisions of the Council, with Calvin's opinions on each appended. Sometimes he wrote in the margin 'excellent', 'good' and, at other times, 'rubbish' and 'nonsense' — but he did not fear to let the exact words of the Council be seen. On this Dr. Theodore W. Casteel writes: "From a purely polemical view this method would seem to have obvious disadvantages. It makes accessible to one's readers not only one's own views, but also those of one's opponents. But it was a method Calvin used many times". It was a sad day for Irish presbyterianism to find so many members of Assembly were afraid of academic freedom. I hope none of those who opposed the Faculty's action feared that the Faculty would have betrayed Reformed doctrine or that our students were of such feeble intellect they would be led astray.

This event had a rather peculiar effect so far as I was concerned. Up to this I normally had been invited to preach some ten or twenty Sundays each year. From June 1966 onwards, for some six years, only one man asked me consistently each year to preach for him, the Rev.W.M. Boland of Malone, and my yearly invitations never exceeded three. I think I must have been thought responsible for the invitation. I acknowledge freely that it had my full approval. Things returned to normal in 1972-73, but I have never been able to fathom why — for I still approve.

In 1960, it was my turn to become warden. This involved me in all sorts of things which had nothing to do with Church History — certifying the domestic accounts each month, getting the coke furnace serviced, having the organ voiced, getting the correct flavouring for the Christmas pudding, and such matters. It brought me into close contact with the matron, cook, domestic staff, and janitors. My aim was to make the whole college a family and in this the Faculty, the students, Miss Rose Thompson (matron) and her staff all played a positive role. Miss Thompson retired in 1975 and was succeeded by Miss Valerie Carson. She is a great personality. As one student put it, "she has her wee ways, but she is the most caring person imaginable". She is also efficient. I remember her coming to me at the end of her first year to report that an inventory had been made of all the college domestic property and that all was accounted for except one teaspoon. Being the culprit, as I had taken it when making a cup of coffee, I had to hand it over.

I saw my task as warden to be a fatherly adviser to the students so this is probably an appropriate place to thank one of them, David Armstrong, for his gracious tribute to me in his *A Road too Wide*. He is over-kind, for I would have done the same for any student. This being understood, let me set modesty aside for a moment and let his words speak for themselves:

Looking back I think that the course I enjoyed most at college was History, and especially the Church History course taught by Professor Barkley — the man I'd been warned about before my arrival at college. I knew that his theological views differed from mine and was very suspicious about him. But as I got to know him better, I realised what a kind and caring man he was. He was a friend to all the students, someone to talk to over a cup of coffee, someone who would remember to ask after your wife. He seemed to be interested in us as people, and this impressed me very much.

In 1964, I became Vice-Principal and Secretary. This meant that the main administrative work fell on my shoulders. The office of Principal by tradition went to the senior professor, which I became in 1976. This was a particularly busy period. The union of ACB and MCD had to be steered through, and a scheme for working together *pro tem* prepared. A Bill had to be drafted for Parliament. A complete survey of the origins and terms of all the College endowments had to be drawn up. Many of them had to be cleared with the Department of Finance or in the High Court. Where MCD funds were involved Principal J.S. McIvor was a tower of strength and a dependable authority. Needless to say I sighed with relief when The Union Theological College of the Presbyterian Church in Ireland Act 1978 received the Royal Assent. On 1st October, 1977, I began a study of wills, problems, minutes of trustees and General Assembly on the College's endowments and finances. In fact, it was Christmas Eve before I completed this. Having read nothing else for three months, boys! was I glad when it was finished.

We had a regular intake of students from abroad. In my college days, the overseas students were mostly Czechoslovak, Hungarian, Swiss, Dutch and Spanish. In my own year there was Charles Czegledy, a Czech, who became professor of Hebrew in Budapest, and Josef Hornych, a Hungarian. I remember the latter well. I was sent to call him for a meal the day he arrived. He knew no English. I knew no Hungarian. So, I had to summon him in Latin. In my days as a professor, sadly we hadn't a single Czech: rooms were reserved for them, but they received no *visas*. We had three Hungarians, but theirs was a sad story — two were exiles, and the third, Istvan Kardos had had to flee from his homeland after the Revolution in 1956.

We also had one Dutch, one French, several Swiss and Germans, and two Spanish. All were maintained out of the Maxwell Bequest. Originally, it provided for two students each year but, in the late sixties, owing to the fall in its value, I had to reccomend that we take only one student every two years. So, while the occasional Continental student still appeared, the overseas students came mostly from the West Indies, India, and Africa, mostly Malawi. Down the years the Spanish students created a difficulty for us in that having experienced 'religious freedom' they did not return to Spain under Franco, but instead went to America or Australia. This meant that in a way we became an agent robbing the Reformed Church in Spain of its best scholars. Nowadays each student is required to give an undertaking to return to the Church from which he came.

Before we pat ourselves too warmly on the back about the 'religious freedom', let us not forget the case of José. He was a brilliant scholar and very friendly. The Presbytery of Belfast had held a Visitation in the congregation in which he was Assistant. It recommended that steps be taken to increase the number of communicants. The Session entrusted this to José. He ran a special class for some twenty young people, but when it came to the crunch none of them was prepared to become a communicant. They said they went to the pictures or smoked or went to dances, and maintained that if they appeared before the

Session they would be forbidden to do these things.

The following Sunday, José mentioned this in his sermon and said that, in Spain, with all its persecution and restrictions, all that was ever asked of a catechumen was, 'Do you believe in Jesus Christ as your Redeemer and Lord?' and maintained that that was central and all that needed to be asked anywhere. The result? Dark mutterings and outrage. The minister was called home from his holiday that afternoon, the Session met on Monday and José was given ten minutes to say farewell the following Sunday morning.

I wanted to fight this, but could not get any support. "He's not one of our students, you know... "! "It would be different if he was one of our own", I was told.

Would it? I'm not so sure.

The home student body has radically changed also. The easiest difference to discern is that many of them now are married. We had only one female student and her name isn't even listed in Dr. Allen's history. In my final two years as Principal we had Miss Ruth Patterson, Miss Joan Barr, and Mrs Jean Mackarel, now ministers in Seymour Hill, Garnerville and Cavan respectively. Since then the number has increased.

There used to be two sayings about the Ministry in presbyterianism. The first was that it was the aim of every minister to produce a minister to carry the torch after he had laid it down. The second was that every Ulster farmer's hope was to educate one of his sons for the Ministry. God has been good to me in that he gave me one son in Drumreagh, one son in Ballybay and three sons in Cooke Centenary.

In my student days, there were six ministers' sons in the year ahead of mine, four and a grandson in mine, and seven sons in the year following. While holding no brief for ministers' sons, I think there is surely something wrong with a Church which does not attract the sons of her ministers into the Ministry. The same applies to the medical, teaching, and other professions. It is a long time since sons of the manse have been entering the Ministry in similar numbers. The Farm Labourers Act altered the position with regard to farmers' sons. Under it a farm labourer ceases work at 6 p.m. on Friday and does not return until Monday morning, but the cows have still to be milked, they calve, the pigs have to be fed and the horses, the sheep break out, and so on. The result of this legislation has been that in many cases the son, who in former days would have been given to the Ministry, was now provided with a bungalow and kept on the farm. I regard this as a serious loss because of the innate integrity, stubbornness and independence of the Ulster farming stock. In the years 1920-40 a fair number of the students came from Saorstat Éireann. Today the balance between rural and urban has altered and few come from the Republic of Ireland. The whole source structure has changed radically.

In conclusion let me refer to one of the great events in College life, the Carol Service and Christmas Dinner. There was no such thing in my day, and it was a great step forward. On these occasions Rose and Valerie and the domestic staff excelled themselves as did Ian M'Master with his kilt and bagpipes. Each year a guest speaker was welcomed. Some of these were masters of wit like Professor John Faris, Dean of the QUB Faculty of Theology, some were fine story-tellers like the Rev. David Alderdice (Wellington Street).

One sticks out in my memory. His name is Werner Heubeck, who was probably invited more for his bravery in carrying bombs off buses than for his work as a transport supremo. He told of how in his youth, he had been an agnostic if not an atheist. He spoke about the faith of his father and mother — of how he had seen them penniless in the street owning only the clothes they stood up in, and of how their faith in Christ had upheld them and helped them to cope. This ha led him to think "Maybe there's something in it after all"; and how this had led him to face up to the realities of Christianity. So long as I live I will never forget the simple sincerity of that speech. It excelled anything I could ever hope to say. Integrity is essential to faith.

I retired in 1981 and was succeeded by my good friends Professor R.F.G. Holmes as professor of Church History, and Professor E.A. Russell as Principal. I was presented with a cheque, the students gave me a portable television, matron put on a special meal, and Agnes the cook, baked a cake the top of which was iced as a football pitch with goalposts, ball, and the Reds. They were good days, even if at times I felt a bit unsure about the future for my work had become my hobby. However, I need not have worried. As I soon discovered, when one retires, there is more to do than there is time to do it.

8 Service and dissent

Episcope or pastoral oversight in presbyterianism is exercised through Church Courts — Kirk Session in the congregation, and the higher Courts of Presbytery, Synod, and General Assembly. The greatest office of oversight the church can confer is to elect one to become Moderator of the General Assembly. I was nominated for this position in 1977, however, as I was then too deeply involved in the amalgamation of ACB and MCD I had to decline.

As the work of the Church is as wide as life there are a great variety of activities to oversee. One of the most responsible tasks to which one may be appointed is to be convener of a vacancy. This means seeing that the congregation is being supplied with Ordinances and pastoral ministry, and taking steps to fill the vacancy. In this one has to be completely objective and have absolutely no self-interest. You had to encourage the congregation to choose the right man without favouring anybody. I was appointed convener of the vacancy in Nelson Memorial on the Shankill Road in 1959. I had been convener of a commission dealing with the relationship of the congregation and the Taggart Memorial Hall. When this had been settled, the congregation asked to have me appointed convener, "for though we don't agree with him he'll give us a square deal".

This Church was built to the glory of God in memory of the Rev. Isaac Nelson, who wrote *The Year of Delusion* about the Revival of 1859; and later resigned his charge to enter Parliament as a Nationalist to fight for the civil rights of our presbyterian ancestors and of the Ulster people. Its minister at this time had been the Rev. Robert Milford, a man of great culture and a brilliant orator. I heard him preach twice. He stood there with all the dignity and magnetism, grace and power of an outstanding Shakespearean actor: although, indeed, he was very deaf.

While I had visited the like of Malvern Street as a student in the Thirties this was my first experience of ministering on the Shankill, and poor and deprived as it was, I was glad not to find the hunger and destitution of my days on the Donegall Road. Nelson Memorial was a faithful congregation of Christian people set in the midst of a large non-churchgoing population. Its members were friendly independent people, and we got on famously. Then came the crunch. One night at the Session I was asked, out of the blue:

"Would you accept a Call if we recommend you to the congregation?"

This took me by surprise so I asked for a week to think it over. My reply was in the negative, but when I look at what they have been through, I sometimes wonder if I made the right decision. Of one thing I am sure, namely that the friendship I received in Nelson has sustained me over the years, and that to this day I am glad to number the Rev. Noel Williamson (QUB) among my friends. I had also to visit New Barnsley. This was a new estate, grass was cut, windows were washed, gutters were cleaned, woodwork was painted. Everything was neat and tidy and the people were good neighbours. Tragically, during the troubles, the people have been driven out of their homes and one would hardly recognise the area today.

My second and third convenorships were given to me by the Presbytery of East Belfast. Both were in First Ballymacarrett. Nelson Memorial and First Ballymacarrett were not only very good to me but for me. This work eliminated any possibility of my getting lost in academia. For a professor to take on convenership after convenership would be quite wrong. At the same time, to have this responsibility once every ten or twelve years keeps one's feet firmly on the ground. I know it was good for me.

My work with the Boy's Residential Club had a similarly bracing effect. There was no place here for professorial airs. The club had been formed by the Rev. W.J. Thompson (College Square) in his own home. His epitaph is written not in pen and ink, but in transformed lives. It moved to Windsor Avenue and then to Black's Road. A friend asked if I would maybe help out here in 1962 and I ended up visiting it three nights a week for about fourteen years.

The Boys had either been in gaol or borstal, or taken from the Courts. Every boy in the club came from a broken home. There were generally about fifteen to twenty in residence. They were great lads. There was no side or hypocrisy. They were quite straight with one. If they thought you should go to hell, they did not hesitate to send you. With all their hardness everyone of them had a soft spot, but you mustn't let him know you knew it. Take the case of Robert. He had just returned after a few months in Mountjoy for hitting a civic guard. Two days later, he was found by a nurse standing in the middle of a women's ward in the RVH holding a bunch of flowers. If anyone in the club had known about it he would have been mocked for ever after. Yet here was this hard young man (and he was) standing in the ward holding a bunch of flowers for the Warden's daughter, who had had her appendix out, because the Warden's wife "was the only mother I ever had". Sometimes when things went wrong people asked, "How do you stick it when a boy does well for years then goes overboard and lets you down?" As I saw it the boys belonged to one or other of two categories — those who could stand on their own feet or those who would always need a stake. For the latter, I held that while they were in the club, it was the stake. So I sought to discover where the stake had broken rather than to feel let down. I knew they would need a stake throughout their lives. After they left the club it might be a good friend, a good employer, a good wife, but a stake they had to have.

When I went to the club I wore a collar and tie, not clericals, because I knew real influence had to be based on personal relationships, not office. But one evening as I went into the club, Davy sidled up to me:

"You're a minister. You're a minister!".

"Who told you that?", I said.

"I followed you".

I expect Davy did not keep his discovery to himself and that the whole club was told. However, my position had been won and so this failing was never mentioned.

The boys were expected to go to Church, but there was no compulsion. If I went out on a Sunday the first question was, "Are you going to Church?". Then began a search for a white shirts. You couldn't go in a coloured shirt. It had to be white. So, off I would go with some nine or ten white shirted individuals to the service, some of them with no collection. At lunch, they freely expressed their opinion of the Service, especially if there had been a soloist. This was a real eye-opener. They could be scathing. I will never forget their ridicule of one children's address about a mammy mouse and a baby mouse who lived next door to a brewery. One day the mammy mouse found the baby mouse drunk, and made it promise never to drink again. The next day, however, the baby mouse was again found drunk. When the mammy asked,

"Why did you break your promise to me?"

The baby mouse said, "But mammy that was no promise".

"Why?"

"Because I made it when I was drunk".

So boys and girls you should not make promises when you are drunk".

This kept them entertained for the whole afternoon.

Each year we went for a fortnight's holiday. One year it was to Inverkip in Scotland, where I carried Eddie across my shoulders like a sheep on to the Ardrossan boat. Or it might be Co. Wicklow, where on the first night it took almost an hour and a quarter to put up the two tents. Not one of them had the foggiest idea. However, by the time we got to Shankill a week later it was possible to do this in twelve minutes. I often spent the morning of Christmas Day here, helping Santa Claus to distribute the presents and enjoying a dinner of turkey and plum pudding with crackers.

Every boy was expected to work and to contribute according to his means. But for some it was not easy to find a job. At times, one formed a rather low opinion of society. Let us take the case of Willie. He was twenty-three and had the IQ of a six year old. He could not be let go to buy anything on his own. Eventually he got a job in a hotel. After a while he asked the warden if he could start a cigarette shop in the club — his idea being to break a packet and sell the cigarettes one at a time at 2d each. The warden forbade this, however, a week later Willie appeared with 600 cigarettes. Now when a boy with no money appears with 600 cigarettes something odd is going on. We looked into it and discovered that he had taken them from the hotel. He was then told he would have to return or pay for them. The warden went to see the manager and received a glowing report about Willie and his work. At this, the warden said that Willie had something to tell him. Willie confessed, apologised and paid for the cigarettes. The manager assured both of them that the matter was closed. Both left believing that 'honesty is the best policy'. That was Monday. On Friday Willie received his cards.

A storm broke out at the club:

The warden and I were mugs. 'Honesty does not pay'. 'Everyone is against us'. 'No-one'll give us a chance'. There was over a good month's discontent. Of course, what did the damage was not the sacking. It was the sacking *after* the assurance that there would be no sacking. This may be an extreme case, but all too often it is well nigh impossible to find a place within society for offenders. They get too easily written off.

I often think of Freddie, Dinger, Sam, Davy, George, Adair, Robert, and the others, left without a home when the club was burned down by 'republican elements' in 1974, and rejoice today in the fact that it has been possible to renew this work with young offenders in Thompson House which perpetuates the memory of the Rev. W.J. Thompson.

In 1948 I was appointed convener for secondary education. This involved me in preparing a Service for St. Patrick's Day and Prayers from Irish Sources for the Northern Ireland schools edition of *Daily Service,* edited by Canon G.W. Briggs. In the Service for St. Patrick's Day, I had included the Lord's Prayer with the rubric: "The children should be taught to say the Lord's Prayer together, slowly and reverently". When submitted to the Board, a Moderator of the future objected: "Presbyterians do not say the Lord's Prayer. That will have to be omitted". Omitted it was. I'll not record what I thought.

It also involved regular meetings with the Minister of Education, Harry Midgely, and the Prime Minister, Lord Brookeborough. The situation I inherited was not a happy one. The Church's previous dealings with the Northern Ireland government had been *ad hoc* and unminuted, which allowed the government to renege on what the Church had taken to be promises. We felt we were getting something of a raw deal. So on our second meeting, when, after some polite chat and tea, the Prime Minister asked:

"What is it you *really* want?"

I replied, "I have it set out here",and reached him and the Minister typed copies. At which the PM said to the Minister,

"This is something new. A deputation from the Presbyterian Church which knows what it wants".

This made me mad, and from then on I drew up a memo of every meeting, sending them a copy to be initialled and returned. There was no more jiggery-pokery after that.

Or rather there was just one piece. At a meeting with Harry Midgely, the Moderator and I had been assured of the introduction of a measure setting aside of 10% of grammer school places for those who, for whatever reason, had failed their Eleven Plus. I went up to Stormont to hear the reform announced in Harry's speech. He made no mention of it. Afterwards I met him in the corridor, confronted him with his breach of promise, and demanded a meeting of the Cabinet at half past nine the following morning. Otherwise, I told him, I would go to the press.

"We control the press."

"I don't mean the *Telegraph* or the *Newsletter*. I'm going to the English press to tell them you lied to the Moderator and myself."

We got our meeting, seeing Harry, the PM and the Minister of Finance, while the other members of the cabinet loitered in the corridor. The measure was announced on the wireless that night.

I think Dr. J.A.H. Irwin (Lucan) hoped that I would eventually succeed him as convenor of the Government Committee, the person to whom the governments in both parts of Ireland referred in Church matters. He did much to protect the standing and rights of the Presbyterian Church in Éire in a very disturbed and at times hostile environment. In my various dealings with government I learned a considerable amount about the politicians themselves. I found the southern to be generally devious and the northern to be always looking over their shoulder.

I remember my father saying to someone when I was a child:

"You know, when we were in Malin our next door neighbours lived in America".

The connection was a strong one and I think this is probably the origin of my interest in that country. This, of course, was cemented by a study of the part played by Mackemie, Hampton, Rogers, Hutcheson, Alison, Thompson and a whole host of ordinary folk in its founding. So in 1949, when the Rev. Dr. J.F.B. Carruthers addressed the Assembly and proposed the formation of "an Irish-American Foundation or Council of friendship". I rejoiced in being appointed a member. In 1952, I had staying with me Dr. Ralph W. Lloyd, President of Maryville College, Tennessee, and later Dr. Roberts, Dean of Princeton Theological Seminary and both were invited to address the Assembly's ICR Board.

This was about all that happened. The next year the committee's existence came to an end. Had this opportunity been cultivated Irish presbyterianism might have been subject to much less misrepresentation and lying propaganda in America during the past twenty-five years. So I welcome Josiah Beeman's recent proposal on behalf of the American Presbyterian General Assembly to form an Inter-Church Committee on Northern Ireland. My reason may be expressed in the title of an American pamphlet on Religious Liberty — *Brewed in Scotland, Bottled in Ireland, Uncorked in America.*

The stir created by Karl Barth's *Baptism* of 1943 and the fear of indiscriminate baptism gave rise to much anxiety and debate within the Church. Barth held that only believers should be baptised, excluding children. The implication of this, as I pointed out when I reviewed the book, is that there is both a God of the Old Testament who includes children in His Covenant, and a God of the New Testament who does not. Barth implied a belief in two Gods, a heresy condemned in the third century. However Barthism was then all the go, and the question of baptism was frequently raised in the General Assembly.

In view of the number of times it has been raised, one would have thought that the entire Church would have been adequately informed as to our position. Yet in 1987 the Irish Mission again raised the issue of re-baptism. Re-baptism has always aroused particular concerns. Having considered the Biblical evidence, the teaching of the Westminster *Confession of Faith* "and in the light of the reports received by the General Assembly", the Doctrine Committee declared against re-baptism. This also applies to converts from other denominations. Even Henry Cooke, whose theology was sounder than his ploitics, would not re-baptise converts. People are baptised into the Christian Church, not a denomination.

I also believe in baptising the children of believers. Because I am absolutely convinced of this, in the light of today's criticisms, I must set out my belief. No one rejected the baptism of infants as an apostolic practice until Peter de Bruys, a medieval heretic who died c.1140. You ask, 'What about Tertullian?' Let us look at what Tertullian actually says:

Baptism is not rashly to be administered... And so, according to the circumstances and disposition, and even age of each individual, the delay of baptism is preferable; principally in the case of little children (*cunctatio baptismi utilier est*). Why does the innocent period of life hasten to the 'remission or sins' (in baptism)? For no less cause must the unmarried be deferred, in whom temptation is prepared... and in the widowed by means of their freedom, until they either marry or the flames of passion have died in them... If any understand the weighty import of baptism, they will fear its reception more than its delay...

Tertullian is sometimes quoted as opposing infant baptism. It is more correct to say he did not 'favour it because of his doctrine of post-baptismal sin. There was no hope of salvation if one committed even one sin after baptism: "The door of forgiveness has been shut and locked with the bolt of baptism". On this question, Tertullian follows *The Pastor* of Hermas, when he adds, God:

still allowed some opening to remain. He has stationed in the vestibule a second penitence to open to them that knock; but only once, because it is a second time; it can never open again, because the last time it opened in vain...

Because of this doctrine, Tertullian wrote as he did. Thank God that, in reply to Peter's question, "Do I forgive my brother seven times?", Jesus answered, "I do not say to you seven times, but seventy times seven". If that wasn't true, there wouldn't be much hope for some of us. Tertullian, however, does teach us one thing. He points to St. Mark x, 13-16 being the warrant for infant baptism. This shows its authority is not in the use of the word 'baptism' in a particular text, but in the nature and character of God in Christ.

Sometimes today when parents seek baptism for their child the determining factor is their spiritual competence, whether they are saved or regular church-goers or something else. That they may still retain a feeling for the Church and for what it stands, and have an instinctive sense of the importance of baptism, is completely ignored. Indiscriminate baptism admittedly is not likely to lead to Christian maturity. But it is even more improbable in the child and family after being turned down by the Church. For example, in the case of an unmarried mother it can mean that the child rejected in the wider community is finally rejected by the last bastion of mercy, compassion and hope — the Church. There is need for a lot of hard thinking here.

How do I approach it? The New Testament affirms that all things in creation are "in Christ", irrespective of whether this is subjectively acknowledged or not. Baptism declares the way things truly are "in Christ":

The world, fallen and marred by evil is still God's world. And God in Christ has claimed the universe as his... every man and every new-born baby is in Christ, is claimed and saved by the Cross and Ressurection of Christ... Baptism is a declaration... and assurance that the love of God, the reign of Christ, the dispensation of the Holy Spirit are a fact in spite of all appearances...

This means that the nature of baptism is not reducible to its functions. This theology is truly Reformed. At baptism I believe the vital question is "This child was made by Christ. What can I, the Session and congregation best do that he or she may come to experience this personally?" For this reason I introduced into the baptismal rite, a vow to be taken by the congregation in 1965. This was an absolutely new practice in Irish presbyterianism.

I further believe that moments of deep distress should never be used for scoring theological points. I am thinking here about times at childbirth when the child or perhaps the mother is dying. I always thought it was my Christian duty to *minister,* not to win theological arguments. If the mother is dying and she asks that the child be baptised, do so and let her pass away satisfied. You can talk it over later with the father. If it is the child who is dying, minister to the parents' sorrow. Baptise the child. You can talk it over with them later.

In presbyterianism, the discipline of baptism is the responsibility of the Session. To celebrate the sacrament of baptism is to minister to people. It is *people* who are baptized, not things. Parents are entitled to have their children baptised on profession of faith in God in Christ, not on the personal idiosyncrasies of individual ministers — or Kirk-Sessions.

The Church has always claimed the right to determine her own doctrine. The state has not always recognised this right, so the necessity to ask parliament to recognise the Church's claim was debated. I felt this to be vital. In 1968, the General Assembly resolved that:

in view of certain ambiguities and uncertainties regarding the meaning of subscription to the Westminster *Confession of Faith,* the Assembly direct the Judicial Commission to consider the manner in which the church is legally bound to the detailed text of the Westminster Confession, and other related legal matters, and report.

Counsel's opinion was sought. It stated:

In my opinion, there is no escape from the conclusion that the Church, by the Act of 1840, must be held to have accepted the text of the Westminster Confession as setting out in carefully selected words, but in as short a form as possible, the fundamental doctrines of her faith, the whole of which faith was contained in the Scriptures of the Old and New Testaments... There is no uncertainty in my mind that the Westminster *Confession of Faith* in the affairs of the Church occupies the position of a subordinate standard of the Church's faith, which contains the fundamental doctrines of that faith. This seems to follow logically from the Act of 1840, the Rule of Faith, and the Minutes of the Assembly referred to on page 5 of *The Code*. It also seems to accord with Dr. Barkley's conclusion to the second of his Carey lectures... I think any uncertainty there is can be removed, and I think as in Scotland it should be removed by both Church and Parliamentary legislation... There is no doubt but that the Church has always had a power to do that judicially... This is a matter clearly within the competence of the Church... I am not at all satisfied that the Church *ex proprio motu* is empowered... to issue declaratory statements as to the sense in which she understands the Westminster Confession except in making a judicial decision... I consider there are limitations on the Church's right to interpret and explain the *Confession of Faith,* and that she has no power to alter or modify it.

I was interested to find Counsel's opinion confirming my own. What this opinion means is that the General Assembly is only able to "interpret and explain her articles of faith judicially", and that all trusts, property, etc. are tied to the *verba ipsissima* of the Westminster *Confession of Faith.* In the light of this, the Judicial Commission decided to attempt to draw up Declaratory Articles.

In 1972, the Assembly sent the matter down to presbyteries inviting their decision on "enabling legislation". The replies were inconclusive so, in 1973, the whole question of Declaratory Articles was withdrawn.

This was the saddest day in the whole of my ministerial career — to find that my Church, which always claimed to stand for the crown rights of the Redeemer in His Church, was not prepared to fight for civil recognition of this. I recorded my dissent and asked that my reasons be minuted. They are reproduced in Appendix A and have never been answered.

My membership of the General Assembly's Inter-Church Relations Committee (now, Board) between 1948-80 fully involved me in Ecumenical issues. I accept Ephesians 4. 1-7, I Corinthians 12-13, and St. John 17. 20-23 as the Biblical basis for Christian unity. In January, 1983, when four Russian Orthodox leaders visited Ireland from a larger delegation to the British Isles, I had the honour of presiding as chairmen of the ICC at a Praise Service in Fitzroy Church. I was saddened by a small protest describing our visitors as "communist agents". No doubt the protesters were sincere, but they forgot that many Christians have for the most part to live under regimes not of their making. They forgot that the Orthodox Church in Russia has given more martyrs for Christ in the twentieth century than all other churches put together. They also forgot there is a thing called good manners.

I also had the pleasure of welcoming at a service in Fitzroy the Rev. Luis Palau, the distinguished Argentinian evangelist; and of receiving Church leaders from the Soviet Union, led by Metropolitan Sergel of Odessa and Kherson. Such meetings, along with visits from Scotland, Wales and England, did much to help widen our perspectives.

As we know to our cost, talks on church unity in Ireland have always failed. This has not been for want of trying. We and the Congregationalists have produced Agreed Statements on our Common Faith and Practice. The Methodists were invited into and joined this process in 1964. We worked well together and in the following year produced Agreed Statements on Scriptures, Creeds and Confessions. When the Church of Ireland was invited in, however, the Congregationalists withdrew. The Church of Ireland was at first rather cagey, but soon the Tripartite Talks as they were known, produced Agreed Statements on a wide range of matters. The main sticking point was the question of the creation of a mutually recognised ministry. Following the Lambeth Quadrilateral in 1920, the General Assembly recognised that union without a mutually recognised ministry is impossible. This I believe to be correct. The problem is to achieve this, and the scheme suggested by the Tripartite Talks, 'Towards a United Church', was considered not to do so. The Reports from the Presbyteries on it in 1974 were either lukewarm, apathetic, or hostile, not only to these proposals but to the general idea of Church Union. I believe this arose from a serious lack of concern with the Biblical call to a unity which is not only spiritually real but also evident in the way the Church is ordered. In other words, that the Churches must not only be one, but seen to be one.

The Tripartite Negotiations stalled, and though they continued for another decade, there was little progress. Regrettably the General Assembly withdrew from them in 1988.

In 1985 the British Council of Churches, of which the Presbyterian Church in Ireland is a member, began an Inter-Church process entitled 'Not Strangers but Pilgrims' began in the BCC. In this Anglican, Baptist, Congregational, Lutheran, Methodist, Orthodox, Pentecostal, Roman Catholic and Reformed Churches participated. They set forth their proposals in a booklet entitled *Next Steps for Churches Together in Pilgrimage*. In this process, the Irish Churches were observers. This Report was placed before the General Assembly in 1989 when it was proposed that:

the Presbyterian Church in Ireland agrees to participate in the proposed ecumenical body for Britain and Ireland as a full member church.

The resolution was defeated by 453 votes to 289, with approximately 100, including myself, recording their dissent. The Church is divided, and there is need for understanding and charity.

Since the mid-sixties, a sinister fundamentalist separatism had been growing within Irish presbyterianism (with its roots in Paisleyism and Orangeism) which led to the formation within the church of the Campaign for Complete Withdrawal. As one of its leaders said, "Our aim is to get the Church out of the WCC this year, and then out of the BCC and ICC". I believe there is need for vigilance if Irish presbyterianism is not to become an isolated self-centred body. By 1990, the Presbyterian Church in Ireland had ceased to be a member of the WCC, of the Tripartite Talks, of the Council of Churches of Britain and Ireland, and had only remained a member of the Irish Inter-Church Meeting by four votes.

Irish fundamentalists appear to me to read the New Testament with different eyes from, for example, Professor F.F. Bruce, the distinguished conservative-evangelical scholar, who declares that "Separation from one's fellow-Christians is contemplated with nothing but horror in the New Testament".

Street-demonstrations as well as party-political denunciation against the Presbyterian Church in particular became a feature of Ulster religious life. Because of this, one Inter-Church Relations Board report to the Assembly opened with the words: "In Northern Ireland at least, it seems we are never for long without an 'ecumenical crisis' of some kind". At times, the police even had difficulty in protecting members of Assembly and their guests. The abuse did not come from Roman Catholics but from those who described themselves as 'born-again' Christians.

Opposition to ecumenism was organised in Northern Ireland by both politicians and fundamentalists. It was bitter and vitriolic. The attack on the Presbyterian Church was vicious and some individuals were harassed. I will mention two events that seem to me to be symptomatic.

On the Twelfth of July, 1966, the Orange Order made a vicious attack upon the Churches. Its official resolution constituted a deliberate attempt by a political organisation to interfere in the life of the Church. Because of the resolution's distortions and misrepresentations, I, as chairman, and Rev. David Turtle, as secretary, wrote on behalf of the Belfast Council of Churches to Captain Sir George A. Clark, Bt., D.L., Grand Master of the Grand Lodge of Ireland, inviting him to meet us. He replied that he was unable to do so "as he had fallen off his horse". There was no suggestion that he was prepared to meet us on a future date. What would have happened if King William had had a similar accident before the Battle of the Boyne?

A further scandal was the cancellation of the service and meetings in St. Anne's Cathedral at which the Bishop of Ripon, who had been an observer at Vatican II, was invited to speak, as a result of the campaign mounted against him and threatened demonstrations by Paisleyites which gave rise to fears for public order. This led the General Board to issue a statement on civil and religious liberty, condemning the actions of the protesters:

liberty includes the right of individuals or groups to express an orderly dissent... With the exercise of this right, however, goes an equal responsibility to ensure that the dissent or protest is not made in such a way as to lead to an effective loss of freedom of speech or worship because of pressure or intimidation towards those who express unpopular views. To act thus is to strike a blow against Protestant principles, no matter who may be involved. We totally repudiate any attempt to repress civil or religious liberty in our land or to usurp the proper order and discipline of any Church as exercised within its own life and membership.

This statement is in keeping with the blackmouth tradition I recognise as my own. Sadly, even as I write, a visit by the Rev. David Armstrong (formerly Limavady) has had to be cancelled, I understand "because of the threat of Paisleyite demonstrations". This is tantamount to mob rule. It has nothing to do with liberty or dissent.

The year 1971 was one of crisis, and a turning point in ecumenical affairs in Irish presbyterianism. In 1969 the WCC had decided to establish a Program to Combat Racism (PCR), and to set up a Special Fund to assist organisations of the racially oppressed. Grants were made to various political groups and organisations, some of whom used armed force, on the understanding that the money would not be used for military purposes. Some (like myself) saw this as relief work, like grants to Arab and Russian refugees; others saw it as a Church body sending arms and military aid to those who believed in slaughter. In Ireland, beset by gunmen and terrorists for over a century, where murder, maiming, kidnapping and violence are daily occurrences, it is not surprising that the general response was bewilderment and hostility, especially when it was hinted by opponents of the WCC that it had contributed to IRA funds. The PCR Board sought to counteract this sort of innuendo but with little success. People believed what they wanted to believe.

I did not speak out on this issue but I thought it reprehensible that the WCC was incapable of distinguishing between the situation in parts of Africa, and Ireland, where democratic methods are open to all.

In 1975, the Revs. William M. Craig (First Portadown) and R. Dickinson proposed: "That the General Assembly withdraw the Presbyterian Church in Ireland from membership of the World Council of Churches". Rev. R.N. Brown proposed, and Rev. Donald Gillies, seconded, an Amendment:

That the General Assembly withdraw the Presbyterian Church in Ireland from membership of the WCC only if the basis of the WCC is so altered as to deny the fundamental doctrines of the faith confessed by the Presbyterian Church in Ireland and/or its Constitution is so altered as to infringe upon the freedom of our Church to order its own life and witness.

481 voted for and 381 against the latter.

Let me make it quite clear that I believe the WCC was, and still is, open to criticism, and that no-one should object to withdrawing from the WCC had it been for the right reason, for example, if it had denied the doctrine of the Trinity or the Incarnation. This was *not* the right reason. Those responsible for this action describe themselves as 'conservative-evangelicals', but to me they appear to be separatists.

In 1980, when the Rev. R. Dickinson (Tobermore) moved and Rev. Dr. R.E.H. Uprichard (Trinity, Ahoghill) seconded "That the General Assembly rescind its former decisions in regard to membership of the WCC and terminate that membership". After the defeat of an amendment "to adjourn a decision... until after the next meeting of the General Assembly of the World Council... in 1983, and meantime to continue suspension of our membership" had been defeated, I moved the following amendment, seconded by the Rev. S. Wilson (First Bangor):

That the General Assembly of the Presbyterian Church in Ireland affirm their faith in one God, Father, Son, and Holy Spirit; and that the Word of God contained in the Scriptures of the Old and New Testaments is the only 'infallible rule of faith and practice', while holding the Westminster Confession of Faith and Catechisms as their subordinate standards. In this faith and discipline the Assembly give thanks to God for men of Christian vision who challenged the churches to found the World Council of Churches, thus enabling Churches, in spite of their differences, to witness together to the world that they accept Jesus Christ 'as God and Saviour according to the Scriptures', and are prepared to work together in His name 'to assist the Christian community in the proclamation of the Gospel of Jesus Christ, by word and deed, to the whole world, to the end that all may believe in Him and be saved'. The General Assembly accordingly hereby withdraws the suspension of this Church's membership of the WCC and confirms its witness to God in Christ under the guidance of the Holy Spirit as a member Church.

Both of us knew this resolution to be rather long, but believed it was necessary to affirm the doctrinal position of the Presbyterian Church in Ireland, to make clear that the WCC was, in spite of its defects, a Christian vision and that we ought to be part of it. This was defeated by 388 votes for to 448 against and when the original motion was put it carried by 433 votes to 327, the hour of the day having led some members to withdraw. So Irish presbyterianism ceased to be a member of the WCC or to speak with the same voice as the World Presbyterian Alliance on Ecumenism.

I had one law in the debates of Presbytery and Assembly, namely never to speak when I didn't know what I was talking about, a rule, alas, that is not universally observed. I enjoyed the cut and thrust of debate and trust that I was never rude or personal. To me, the Church is a living, dynamic community, and the Assembly must always reflect that positively and constructively, pointing the way forward. To fail to do this is to fail the Church.

9 Progressus ex variis frustrationibus!

It annoys me to hear people talk about "the two traditions in Ireland". There are three — 'Catholic nationalism', the child of ultramontanism; 'Orange-Toryism', the child of the Ascendency; and the liberalism of the Dissenters and Blackmouths. Ultramontanism destroyed the residual liberalism, to which Fergus O'Ferrall pays tribute in his pamphlet *Liberty and Catholic Politics 1790-1990*, within Roman Catholicism; and Orange-Toryism destroyed it within presbyterianism. The former may be dated between the years 1866-90 and the latter 1885-1910. For example, in 1888, Hugh Hanna, a Tory wrote "There are not more than a dozen Conservatives among the 550 members of Assembly". This presbyterian liberal tradition was best seen in men like Richard Smyth, John Kinnear, Macauley Brown, A.P. Gowdy, John MacNaughton and Thomas MacKnight.

The concept of 'two traditions' arises from the liberal tradition's almost complete disappearance after 1886. But it is only applicable in a qualified sense from the end of the first decade of the twentieth century. It could almost be dated to the day in 1913 when, because of the promulgation of the *Ne temere* decree and the M'Cann case, the Assembly voted 921 against and 43 for Home Rule — a very different situation from twenty years earlier, in 1893, when the voting was 304 to 11 with the remarkable number of 341 abstentions. The presbyterians, who within living memory had escaped from an Anglican denial of the validity of their marriages and the legitimacy of their children, were not going to risk receiving the same treatment from the Church of Rome.

The political policy became one of separation. It has resulted in a harsh and bitter hatred which the politicians, both north and south, continue to cultivate. The presbyterian position was:

Opposed as our church has always been to the partition of the United Kingdom, the other partition — between one part of Ireland and another — was never desired by it. It was only reluctantly accepted as the lesser of two evils between which it was necessary to choose...

The two evils were civil war and partition. To avoid the former, if possible, it accepted the latter "for the sake of peace" and "to avoid civil war". In 1925, the General Assembly stated:

We greatly regret that the Boundary Question has been raised at the present time and in the form it has assumed. If local adjustments of the Boundary are thought necessary for the convenience of those who live near the border there could be no objection to their being carried out in a just and friendly way; but we strongly protest against a large section of the Six Counties, given to the Northern Government in the Act of 1920, being wrested from it.

The Assembly's attitude was conciliatory and left room for negotiation. While he was dealing specifically with proposals and schemes, I feel it is a pity that the late Professor John White in his scholarly survey, *Interpreting Northern Ireland*, makes no mention of this.

I sometimes visited a Manse in Co. Donegal where on the mantlepiece in the study was a framed copy of the Ulster Covenant. It had been torn in two and written across it were the words "The broken covenant". At first sight, the writing looked like a dark stain. It had been written in the minister's own blood. He had been a unionist and had been appointed with another to represent the unionists of Donegal at a meeting with Carson at the City Hall in Belfast. Instead of being treated sympathetically, he and his companion were called upon to resign. They refused and were evicted. No longer was it "Ulster Will Fight And Ulster Will Be Right". Donegal, Monaghan and Cavan were to be sacrificed. The night he returned home saw the torn and blood-stained covenant placed on the study mantlepiece where it remained until the day he died.

The betrayal was never forgotten and I saw with my own eyes the anguish of one of those who had been betrayed.

I knew there was also a bitter legacy of distrust on the nationalist side and understandably so. But I did not like the problem's one-sided presentation. Following a TV programme in which a well-known nationalist said that, following the 1920 Act, nationalists did nothing, trusting that the Boundary Commission would give them what they wanted, I decided to write to the producer and point out the disingenuousness of this statement. For by March 31 1922, by murder, burnings-out and terrorism, presbyterian numbers had been reduced in the presbytery of Athlone by 30%, of Connaught by 36%, of Cork by 45%, of Dublin by 16% and of Munster by 44% — not to mention their dead, and the destruction in the nine counties of Ulster. I was told that the the matter would be looked into, but when the series was repeated the scene was re-run without alteration.

I knew the gut hatred this produced. I knew I could not lead a crusade like Bernard of Clairvaux. Anyway, I didn't want that. I realised I would have to work alone and as the opportunity arose.

On the other hand, I knew two other things. They were vital. I knew that relations within and between Church and State were wrong and I believed that through the Holy Spirit they could be changed. In this I was encouraged by my upbringing and, paradoxical as it may seem, by presbyterian history. I knew that there had been a time when a presbyterian minister died, he could be buried in a 'chapel' graveyard and that presbyterian Volunteers paraded and attended the first Mass at the Dedication and Opening of the first Roman Catholic Church, St. Mary's, in Belfast without being regarded as betraying the faith and that there was a time when the Roman Catholic priest of St. Patrick's, Belfast, could attend an Installation in a Presbyterian Church and at the reception afterwards respond to the toast: "Our brethren of the Roman Catholic persuasion", and that presbyterians honoured the toast in something stronger than water, if congregational accounts of the period are to be believed. I knew that most Irish bishops were Gallicans and many priests were educated at Salamanca and elsewhere. I knew also that most presbyterian ministers were educated in Glasgow or Edinburgh. I knew that while there were vital theological differences between presbyterians and Roman

Catholics, they had much in common and were able to live together.

Further, small though it was I knew the friendship and success of the Club in Balnamore. Even having been able to talk, joke and laugh with Father Duffy, the P.P. in Ballybay encouraged me. I was, in no sense, a leader. Rather, I was a responder to opportunity. There are two problems here — first, the political division in the country, and second the theological division.

Let me look at the former. Were there opportunities to heal the division? I think there were. The Government of Ireland Act (1920) was not a work of genius but no one was able to produce anything better. It provided for a Council of Ireland. The Northern Ireland Government appointed its representatives to the Council. The southern did not. While I know it is hypothetical (as my remarks here must be) I do not hesitate to say it would have provided a better opportunity for peace and harmony if they had.

I think there would have been an opportunity for something better had Kevin O'Higgins not been assassinated. He promised in 1925 that the Executive Council of Saorstat Éireann would use "what influence it possessed to induce the Nationalist members in Ulster to take their place in the Northern Parliament". His peaceful intent died with him. The existing border (as in the 1920 Act) was confirmed in a tripartite Agreement signed by the representatives of Dublin, Stormont, and Westminster on 3 December, 1925, since the three governments "united in amity... resolved to aid one another in a spirit of neighbourly comradeship". Saorstat Éireann lodged this with the League of Nations as an International Treaty, but it was set aside unilaterally by Éire in Bunreacht na hÉireann in 1937, which declares "the national territory consists of the whole island of Ireland"; and into it was written the Catholic Social Code derived from the Encyclicals of Pope Pius XI. This widened the gap. Personally, as a blackmouth, while I can respect a Roman Catholic or a presbyterian for being faithful to the ethical teaching of his own church, this is an ecclesiastical matter and ought not to be given legal status in the Constitution. This undermines liberty of conscience and the rights of minorities. It is constitutional discrimination.

The next opportunity to make a positive contribution in the South was probably the 'constitutional crusade' of Garret Fitzgerald. But it was still-born, though it must be said Garret's intentions were of the best. Then came the New Ireland Forum in 1983-84. Over 300 groups and individuals responded to its invitation and made submissions. Though none of the Unionist parties participated, Garret claimed:

The ideas we have put forward together show an openness to the other tradition in this island, and a sensitivity which I believe, has no precedent in Irish History.

But surely Clare O'Halloran is more accurate when she describes it as "an irredentism which had become anachronistic and devalued in its traditional form". The non-participation of the Unionists was unforgiveable in the circumstances. Here we have another missed opportunity.

Several individuals also stand out. One is Dr. Noel Browne, but he never came to leadership and his autobiography was accurately entitled *Against the Tide*. In the Dáil, the man I think who had the most accurate grasp of Northern affairs and the Unionist mind was Conor Cruise O'Brien, but he never was in a position to do anything. He was Minister of Posts and Telegraphs the year it took me over six-and-a-half hours to make a trunk-call from Dungarvan to Coleraine. Another man who showed something approaching vision was Sean Lemass when he came north to meet Terence O'Neill. It took courage on the part of O'Neill to invite him and it took courage for Lemass to come. He ran the risk of being branded as a traitor by the soldiers of destiny.

President Mary Robinson has expressed her hope for better understanding and friendly relations and her willingness, so far as it lies in her power, to advance these. While she has to act constitutionally, it is to be hoped indeed that she will be able to achieve more than her predecessors in improving north/south relations and that, having extended the hand of friendship, she may find it grasped firmly and with sincerity. The ungracious scenes in the Belfast City Council were hardly a positive contribution.

Nor can I overlook the evidence of Professor J.C. Beckett to the Role of the Church Committee of the General Synod, in which he relates how he asked a leading republican to name any Act of the Oireachtas intended to conciliate northern Protestant opinion. He was unable to do so.

Had he asked the same question to a member of the northern

government, he would have received the same answer.

There were opportunities in Northern Ireland too. The first occurred in 1937-38 when W.J. Stewart founded the Progressive Unionist Party, which numbered several distinguished elders of the Presbyterian Church among its members. Do you remember how it was attacked? How it was suppressed? As they welcomed catholics and advertised their meetings in the *Irish News*, they were declared to be men of 'catholic interests' and so unsound on the question of the border. Craigavon described them as wreckers. Their election meetings were broken up (I remember a meeting in Antrim being broken up by thugs, who threw a hatchet at the speaker). Stewart, the builder of Stormont, was found guilty of fraud.

I knew Stewart. In my twenties I met him in my father's home. I remember him speaking to the General Assembly on social questions like housing. Later I was minister in Cooke Centenary Church of which he was a member. His friends and the older members of Cooke were unanimously of the opinion that he had been set up, and that a massive miscarriage of justice had taken place. He had committed the unforgiveable sin of setting up what might have become a rival and more widely-based unionism. It was a threat, so it had to be destroyed. And it was.

Unionist groups worked only within the Protestant community. The Northern Ireland Labour Party, on the other hand, tried to gain support across the divide. Their efforts failed. They never came to power chiefly because the Unionists held the working man's vote through the Ulster Unionist Labour Association, of which J.M. Andrews was chairman. Buckland describes him as a man who was "over-responsive to the Orange Order". Here again there was a failure to achieve co-operation. Then came the O'Neill-Lemass meeting. It was a stout effort but, as John Knox found in his day, the "rascal multitude" was displeased. Hope blossomed, but it was not to be.

There was perhaps one other man who had the ability as a politician to carry co-operation through. Brian Faulkner's strength lay in the fact that he was essentially a pragmatist. In my opinion, however, because of jealousies within unionism, he got his opportunity too late. Whether he would have proved the reconciling leader the province needed, we will never know, thanks to his early death in 1977.

Since the outbreak of the present troubles the two hopeful efforts were the inauguration of the Standing Advisory Commisson on Human Rights and the Executive set up after Sunningdale. It took office on 1 January 1974, and consisted of six Unionist Party of Northern Ireland, four SDLP, and one Alliance member. The DUP, UUC, and Vanguard opposed it and a general strike was called. This event was interesting to me in that I was visiting regularly in the Ballymacarrett and lower Newtownards Road area at that time. On the Thursday, Friday, and Saturday no-one knew whether the strike would be successful. Opinion was very lukewarm. That night, when I listened to Harold Wilson use the term "scroungers", I knew it would be solid. On Sunday morning, when I arrived to conduct public worship, I found it to be so. The Executive fell, but the five months of its existence did show that given goodwill co-operation is possible.

The only other real attempt was the Anglo-Irish Agreement. Its aim was good, but the method of its introduction meant that it would be a dead duck. Another opportunity was lost.

While there may be differences of opinion about some of these opportunities, I hope I have shown that there were and continue to be opportunities even though they are rarely taken. Even Rabbie Burns 'in his cups' had more vision than Irish politicians and churchmen:

> For a' that, and a' that,
> It's comin' yet, for a' that,
> That man to man, the warld o'er,
> Shall brothers be for a' that.

I have no interest in attempting to apportion blame, so let me simply summarise my position.

John Calvin, as well as being a distinguished theologian, was a great social reformer and knew his ecclesiastical and social reforms in Geneva had to have a sound theological basis. From a study of Geneva I realised that if there was ever to be healing in Ireland the philosophical and theological basis had to be sound. This applied not only to inter-church affairs but also to community relationships. Eventually a political solution would have to be found. Clearly this would be a complex process. Statesmen and politicians would have to formulate the political solutions; economists the economic; the churches the religious; and so on. My effort had to be in the fields of theology and ecclesiology, and history and morals, and in all these areas I sought to exercise a critical openness.

I am not a politician in the sense of being a party politician, but I always vote. To get me a secret vote cost my forefathers dear, so I use it. A presbyterian who does not vote at every election is unworthy of those who fought to get it for him. Of course, when one looks at who and what the various parties put up to be voted for, the only thing you can do at times is spoil your paper. At the same time, if someone is doing what you believe to be right you should support them, using the press or whatever platform is available to you.

Throughout my ministry, I had a rule when writing to the papers: never post it until the next day. Consequently, you could count all the occasions I have written to the press on the fingers of one hand. But I did write one political one. It was to the *Belfast Telegraph* on 28 April, 1969. There had been rioting, destruction, lying and maiming in Derry; and four Church leaders, Dr. Farren, Dr. Tyndall, Mr. Morrison and Mr. Kilgore, walked the streets together to meet the people. I thanked them saying:

The Press described their action as 'an appeal for calm'. It was much more. They, in the name of Christ, set the whole community an example of Christian brotherhood... Jesus Christ, in His earthly life proclaimed peace and goodwill to all, but He was rejected. The action of these four Christian leaders could have been rejected. Let me, therefore, thank the people of Derry for their response to it. You have set an example to the whole country.
May the seed of Christian brotherhood that has been planted grow and flourish not only in Derry, but in the whole community.
Yours,
John M. Barkley.

The fall-out was almost immediate. On 6 May the Presbytery of Ballymena resolved:

That the Presbytery... disapproves of individuals sending out private letters, bearing an official address such as Church House or the Presbyterian College and would ask that this practice cease.

The Clerk of Presbytery, as instructed, forwarded a copy to me, and two days later I was told that it referred to the above letter. This depressed me profoundly, and confirmed my opinion that I must henceforth act alone.

Opportunities to do so did arise. For example, when I was asked to address the Ulster Unionist Labour Association I did so, arguing that the Unionist Party could ever become a completely representative party while its Constitution made provision for offical representation of the Orange Order, The County Grand Lodges being able to nominate 122 delegates out of 712 on its Council. While this remains the constitutional position I argued that one-third of the total population felt debarred. The result was interesting. They agreed that unionists at elections should hold public meetings and make other changes, but to the breaking of this link they were completely opposed. We agreed to differ.

It is vital to seek dialogue, and for the political parties in Northern Ireland to speak to each other. In the present circumstances of destruction and intimidation, mutilation and assassination, there is no excuse whatever for not talking. Early in 1982, I received an invitation from The Social Democratic and Labour Party (SDLP) to speak at a Conference on 'Options for a New Ireland' to commemorate the Bicentenary of Grattan's Parliament. I accepted gladly. My subject was 'The Roots of Sectarianism in Ireland', on which I summed up:

Even if we hold different viewpoints on some issues, sectarianism in Ireland has its roots in national relationships and independence, intolerance and ostracism, religion, religious and political desire to dominate, agrarian strife, trade restrictions, Roman triumphalism, Protestant isolationism, political intransigence, party-political chicanery, and social injustice. On these points, I think, we would all agree. The problem is to create a Social Order, which provides for the welfare of all without injustice to minorities, or crushing individual conscience.

I am not a party-politician. At the same time, however, I cannot shun politics: as a Minister of the Gospel, I cannot escape the necessity for seeking a moral social order. I cannot see any possibility of achieving this, except if it is unanimously accepted that no solution is just which shall not include Irishmen of every religious persuasion and none. There is no structural blueprint, but no matter what is the polity it can be a reality only if all men and parties recognise and honour each other's rights. To achieve this is the task of statesmen. Exclusionist politicians, of which we have a surfeit, are by their very nature of no use at all .

I made a vow in 1940, following Mrs Baird's funeral, to work for better inter-church relations. For years I achieved very little. The climate was against dialogue. Attitudes were governed by uncompromising dogma, for instance in 1864, Pope Pius IX published his *Syllabus Errorum* in which he listed as one of "the principal errors of our time" the idea that "Protestantism is nothing more than another form of the same true Christian religion, in which it is possible to be equally pleasing to God as in the Catholic Church". The same icy wind blew from Rome in 1928 in the Encyclical *Mortalium animos* of Pius XI:

There is but one way in which the unity of Christians may be fostered, and that is by furthering the return to the one true Church of Christ of those who are separated from it.

By "true Church" is meant the Church of Rome. In 1948, because the ecumenical movement was leading Roman Catholic and non-Roman Catholic theologians to have discussions together, Rome decided to protect the faithful in the Admonition of the Holy Office, *Cum compertum*. This reminded Roman Catholics that they were forbidden by Canon Law to participate in or organise meetings, especially 'ecumenical' gatherings with non-Roman Catholics at which matters of faith and morals were to be discussed without prior permission being obtained from the Holy See. The Instruction of the Holy Office *De motione oecumenica*, 1949, though officially noting the existence of the ecumenical movement, reiterated the refusal of the Church of Rome to take part in ecumenical meetings. Then Pope John XXIII in 1959 announced his intention to hold an Ecumenical Council and two years later set up the Secretariat for the Promotion of Christian Unity. In Ireland, there was rigid adherence to the teaching of Pius IX, XI, and XII. The Decree on Ecumenism of Vatican II, *Unitatis Redintegratio*, promulgated on 21 November, 1964, opened the door on a day of hope and brotherhood in Christ.

Of course this was only a starting point. But that was more than we had had for the four hundred years prior to 1965, when the churches in Ireland had few dealings with each other. Snobbery, scorn, jealousy, fear were rampant. Polemicists thrived. A visitor from Mars would have had no trouble in agreeing with Tertullian's observation: "See how these Christians love one another".

Great strides have been made since 1964. There were no Inter-Church relations in Ireland at the beginning of the century and no Protestant/Roman Catholic ecclesiastical relations until 1970. However, even before the promulgation of the Decree on Ecumenism, tentative steps had been taken. The Glenstal meetings had begun in June 1964, that is, five months before the promulgation of the Vatican II Decree. About forty scholars drawn from the four main denominations were present. Once born these talks prospered and continue to the present day.

I am sure others, like myself, approached these meetings with caution and a determination that no one is going to get the better of me. However, such was the plain-speaking, honesty and integrity shown on all sides that I can honestly say that today no one approaches issues at Glenstal except in the spirit of seeking to discover what is the mind of Christ on the question under consideration. Discussion is full, free and frank. Among the many subjects studied have been liturgy, baptism, eucharist, Christian education, and the teaching authority in the Church.

Two vital points may be made here. Firstly, on my suggestion, we decided that we should not publish findings after each Conference, and this was agreed. My reason was that it is possible to arrive at a consensus, knowing that there is a general basis of agreement, but if one tries to put this on paper it is difficult at times to find a form of words acceptable to all. The second important fact is the friendships, trust, confidence, and respect that have been built up, enabling the most divisive issues to be discussed without acrimony.

It is essential to remember that Glenstal is a meeting of individuals. It has no ecclesiastical authority. On the other hand, it should not be forgotten that, had it not been for Glenstal, and the later conference modelled upon it at Greenhills, the establishment of the official Ballymascanlon Talks would have been much more difficult. The main strength of Glenstal is its independence and freedom. On the other hand, each side (if one may speak that way) had a definite weakness. On the Roman Catholic side, the Religious Orders were well represented and, after a few years, some bishops gave papers. There was also a good representation of laity of distinction, but there were very few parish priests. On the Protestant, Bishop J.W. Armstrong was a firm supporter. Other bishops and presbyterian

Moderators participated later. Academics attended, and there was also a fair representation of clerics and divines, but few laity. The small numbers of priests and laity sadly means that the critical openness and positive approach of Glenstal has not penetrated, as much as I would like to see, into parishes and congregations.

The Irish School of Ecumenics came into being as a result of the vision of the Rev. Father Michael Hurley, SJ, and was opened in 1970. Interdenominational in character the School of Ecumenics is not an official institution of any Church, or Council of Churches, having as its motto *Floreat ut pereat* (May it flourish in Order to perish), the underlying idea being that of promoting unity and making itself redundant. It has brought members of the Irish Churches into contact with some of the world's leading scholars, and its students have come from many lands.

Through the Irish School of Ecumenics, which has no parallel anywhere else in Europe, perhaps in the world, it is now possible to graduate in ecumenical studies in Trinity College, and to receive a Certificate in Ecumenics in the New University of Ulster. The high standard of scholarship and the excellent collection of ecumenical literature in the library have enriched the Irish churches, though within presbyterianism its influence has been limited. The Roman Catholic, Anglican, and Methodist Churches have the ability to place a minister back into the mainstream of the Ministry without difficulty, should he decide to opt out for a year's study. The Presbyterian Church unfortunately has no way of doing this. It is something to which serious thought should be given. If we are honest, we must admit that we do not know or fully understand how the other works.

This creates difficulties. Cardinal Conway, used to a quarterly meeting of the Irish hierarchy, found it hard to grasp that presbyterianism had to wait until the first week of June each year for a decision. He could not understand the hold up. This had to be explained before joint-work could proceed. There is need for ecclesiological knowledge of each other's ways.

In 1970, the Doctrine Committee, of which I was a member, drew up a Report, later printed as a pamphlet, on The Relation of the Presbyterian Church in Ireland to the Church of Rome. This was an extensive pamphlet discussing the view of the World Alliance of

Reformed Churches; the criticisms and attitudes of the Reformers to the Church of Rome; Irish presbyterianism's recognition of the Orders and Sacraments in the Church of Rome; has Rome changed on salvation, justification, faith, works, Papacy, Church and State, understanding of the Mass and so on? It shows very remarkable new attitudes in the Church of Rome, which we must gladly welcome. These new circumstances require from our Church a readiness to undertake discussion with members of the Church of Rome on matters of civil justice and community welfare and, not less, on our different understandings of the Christian faith. I prepared some of the preliminary studies on the WARC, the Reformers, Irish Churches and Vatican II. These were then drafted and revised in the Committee:

Agreement was almost unanimous that there are proper occasions for common acts of worship... but there was division of opinion among us on participation in prayer for the unity of Christendom and on attendance at Roman Catholic Eucharistic Services.

My view on this is that if faithful Reformed Churchmen like Calvin, Melanchthon, Capito and Bucer, and devout Roman Catholics like Contarini, Gropper, and von Pflug could meet together without compromising their faith in efforts to achieve reconciliation, it is possible for Christians to do so today without being written off as traitors. The question of eucharistic services admittedly does raise problems for some, owing to the dogma of transubstantiation. This has to be respected. On the other hand, I believe one can claim liberty of conscience, at least on the ground, and there are others, that while we may describe the Eucharist, no one can define it.

The decision in 1970 to set up the joint-group on Social Problems by the ICC and the Roman Catholic hierarchy was a significant step in Irish Inter-Church relations. It has reported on drug abuse, housing, the use of alcohol among young people, under-development in rural Ireland, violence, environmental problems, minorities, the H-Blocks, the prison system in the north, among others. What use do the Churches make of all this material? I am afraid the answer is, 'Very little'.

Yet the momentum gathered. In 1972, I was honoured to be invited as an Observer at the fourth Congress of Jesuit Ecumenists at Milltown Park, Dublin. Here again I was fortunate not to be a total stranger

because the Irish Jesuit Provincial and I were Patrons of the Irish
School of Ecumenics. Ignatius Loyola, the Founder of the Jesuits,
saw the Society as a blueprint for the destruction of Protestantism,
yet here we were trying to "bridge the gap between the Christian
Churches through an honest appraisal of what needs to be renewed
and done in the Catholic household itself". The lectures appeared to
me to be historically and theologically honest and to have avoided
special pleading.

This process fulfilled itself in 1973. The year 1973 was epoch
making. The ICC had written to the Irish Roman Catholic hierarchy
concerning a top-level meeting. In response, chiefly owing to the
influence of Cardinal Conway, the member Churches of the ICC
were invited to a joint-meeting "at which the whole field of
ecumenism in Ireland might be surveyed". It was proposed "that the
Assembly warmly welcome" the invitation. There was some
opposition, and this was emended to that they:

would be glad to meet to discuss all matters regarding Church and Community
relationships, especially the problem of inter-church marriages and the
proclamation of the Gospel in Ireland, but excluding the question of Church
Union.

After a lively discussion, this was passed. So the first
Ballymascanlon Talks took place on 26 September, 1973. I was a
member of the group on Baptism, the Eucharist and Marriage. We
mainly discussed the Eucharist. One representative of the General
Assembly interpreted the doctrine in the Westminster *Confession of
Faith* as "Receptionism", thus emptying the Sacrament of the Lord's
Supper of objectivity. To avoid embarrassing public division, I
submitted my resignation to the convener of the Inter-Church
Relations Board, but this was not accepted. This made it very awkward
for me.

The talks were an interesting experience but, sadly, while it received
full media coverage it tended to be presented as a magic-formula for
solving all Ireland's problems. As an utopian Ireland did not come
into being the next day, many regard Ballymascanlon as a failure or
a talking shop. This is grossly unfair. A new Ireland cannot come
into existence by magic. *Metanoia*, change of heart, is necessary.
Ballymascanlon, despite its weaknesses and failures, must continue.

One of the main features of the Ballymascanlon Talks has been the honesty and straightness of all in the discussions, and that, to the surprise of some, it has been possible to have these without rudeness and abuse. The ideas which emerged here must be followed up and lead to action.

As good a tribute as I can pay to this process is to say that my contacts with Roman Catholics became a matter of routine — PACE meetings, conferences in St. Gerard's, meetings at the Columbanus Community, meetings at Milltown Park, meetings at St. Patrick's College, Maynooth, meetings of the Corrymeela Community, Clonard Ecumenical services, the Ballymascanlon Talks, and elsewhere. They merit mention but are too varied to discuss. From them I learned the need for integrity, to avoid distortion, even if unconvinced not to shut the door, to accept light from any quarter, to show a desire for understanding and goodwill, to place the dogmas of the past in their historical setting, and to listen without interrupting.

But there was also friendship. I learned that Roman Catholic bishops and priests are a lot like presbyterian ministers. They are good story-tellers and enjoy a hearty laugh. They can joke at their own expense. Their devotion to God in Christ is sincere and loyal. They are learning what I had to learn, namely, that until we speak as fellow-Christians, there is little hope for full reconciliation. Even though the gain of theological understanding may be slow, in the eyes of the ordinary man our manifest mutual understanding is essential. In 1978, the General Assembly passed the following resolution *nem.con.*:

That the General Assembly encourage our ministers, elders, and Church members, as part of our witness to the Reformed faith, to be more outgoing in their association with the clergy and members of the Roman Catholic Church, and encourage them where possible to study the Scriptures together, and they further urge that the intention of the resolution be discussed in depth at Presbytery level, in order that precise and definite ways may be found to implement this policy.

This has never been rescinded and remains the policy of the Assembly, even though it must be honestly admitted that some have honoured it more in the breach than the observance.

For instance the General Assembly's *Agreements and*

Disagreements of Irish Presbyterianism and Roman Catholicism of 1990 unfortunately opens with 'disagreements', completely contrary to the Assembly's principle, laid down in 1863 that: "In all dealings with Roman Catholics, we begin with our agreements..." Here the introductory sentence is "It is a well established fact that historically, political and cultural, as well as religious differences have distinguished Irish presbyterians and Roman Catholics..." Differences must not be minimised or ignored, but I had rather the opening sentence was "It is not always accurately recognised the extent of what we, presbyterians and Roman Catholics, hold in common". The Report holds to the traditional position:

Presbyterians stand in the tradition of the Reformers, who taught that, in spite of what they attacked as unscriptural teachings and practices in the Roman Church, vestiges of authentic Christian faith remained. Calvin... could write... 'I call them churches, inasmuch as the Lord there wonderously preserves some remains of his people, though miserably torn and scattered, and inasmuch as some symbols of the Church still remain — symbols especially whose efficacy neither the craft of the devil nor human depravity can destroy'.

I cannot talk of friendship and pass over my old friend Tómas O'Fiaich. Tómas was a warm and amiable man. Many knew him only as Cardinal Tomás O'Fiaich. I met him before he was either an archbishop or a cardinal. He was a member of the academic staff and a scholar of integrity who was proud of and thrilled by the accomplishment of the Irish Church during the Dark Ages. He helped me to see that the term 'Dark Ages' does not refer to a dark age, but to an age about which we know so little that it was dark to us. Many wonderful things were happening at that time. I had had frequent contact with Cardinal O'Fiaich's predecessor Cardinal William Conway. For him I also had a great admiration, but the two men were very different.

Cardinal Conway was a Belfast man and a learned canon lawyer. Cardinal O'Fiaich was a country man from South Armagh and an historian. Their specializations illustrate their differences in approach. In one case the solution is seen as a matter of law, whereas in the other people's relationships are central. Cardinal O'Fiaich and I held different viewpoints. But we respected each other. His was the way of friendship and hope.

I do not know whether the Cardinal knew that King William wrote to the Presbyterians in 1692, 'We do expect you will... not allow yourselves to be imposed upon by some Hot Violent Spirits, who would carry you from Moderation and Charity'. On the other hand, he would have agreed that the cause of Protestantism had been undermined and damaged by what Hamilton Magee, convener of the Irish Mission, described as 'coarse, vulgar, and oftentimes most ignorant abuse' of Roman Catholicism. He deplored this as much as I deplored the distorted and abusive statements of some Roman Catholic dignatories. On the other hand, Tomás O'Fiaich's openness, integrity and friendly spirit augured well for healing and a *modus vivendi*.

I was pleased, therefore, when he invited me to preach in St. Patrick's Cathedral, Armagh, during the Week of Prayer for Christian Unity in 1982. The Scripture Readings were I Kings 8. 41-43 from Solomon's Address to the people and Prayer of Dedication of the House of the Lord, to which Gentiles or strangers were to be made welcome; Acts 10. 34-48 relating how St. Peter visited Cornelius and the circumcised "were amazed, because the gift of the Holy Spirit had been poured out even on the Gentiles for they heard them... extolling God"; and St. Matthew 9. 10-13, telling how Jesus sat at table with his disciples and many sinners and the Pharisees asked his disciples "Why does your teacher eat with sinners and Jesus replied: "Those who are well have no need for a physician, but those who are sick... Learn what this means... I came not to call the righteous, but sinners".

Being a presbyterian, I was taken by surprise in the middle of this when there was applause. I appreciated the welcome I received from the people of Armagh that evening. One thing in particular touched me deeply — the lections were read by families, perhaps the father or daughter or mother with the whole household standing round. It was a kind of miniature of what the Church of God should be.

Another invitation that gave me special pleasure came with the visit of Pope John Paul II to Ireland. The Presbyterian Church in Ireland was invited to be represented at a meeting in Dublin on Saturday, 29 September 1979, at which the Pope would have the opportunity of meeting leaders of the Protestant Churches in Ireland.

After some division, Dr. A.J. Weir, Clerk of the General Assembly wrote accepting. I was honoured to be invited, as Principal of Union Theological College. The Pope addressed us in friendly terms and was then introduced personally to each of the Protestant representatives and the meeting concluded with everyone joining together in offering up the Lord's Prayer.

Later, someone sent me a framed photograph of the Pope and myself shaking hands. You will by now, I suspect, be familiar with it. I did not know it had been taken, and I do not know who sent it to me, so here let me say 'Thank you'. I did appreciate it and hung it up in my study in the College. It was interesting to watch the faces of students when they saw it for the first time.

On such occasions, the required protocol means that there can be no 'exchange of views'. So, it was decided to send to the Pope through the Papal Nuncio in Dublin an Address, together with a number of official reports of the General Assembly, specially bound. In February, 1980, Dr. Weir received a reply in which the Pope spoke of being deeply moved by the Address presented to him and of the happiness it brought to him to know of the serious dialogue between the World Alliance of Reformed Churches and the Roman Catholic Church. He also said he was glad to learn of the dialogue taking place in Ireland between the Protestant and Roman Catholic Churches and hoped that the long and sad history of mutual suspicion and distrust would be overcome.

There are serious theological and other differences between presbyterianism and Roman Catholicism. I know that. It is not to be denied, but if I have been able to do even a little to enable us to live together in harmony, I thank God. I think also of the words "on the Divine Spirit" of that deeply devotional man, Archbishop William Temple:

Always the breath — the wind — of the Spirit is moving. We know it by its effect. We have no need to ask for its authentication — Is it Protestant? Is it Catholic? Where the fruit of the Spirit is apparent, there the spirit is at work. We should place ourselves in its course that we may be carried by its impulse, even though this leads us to association with strange comrades.

At this point, it might be no bad thing to attempt to state where we actually are. In 1964, ecclesiastically Roman Catholics and presbyterians were not even speaking to each other. *A New Catechism,* published by the Roman Catholic Church in 1967, says:

It is impossible to estimate the immense amount of goodness and holiness which the Reformation... has to offer all Christianity. The Catholic Church cannot do without the Reformation... The Reformers did not fight for a chimera.

Instead of the terms 'heretical' and 'schismatic' Vatican II prefers 'ecclesial communities' and 'separated brethren' enabling a positive evaluation to be placed upon the life and worship of other churches. It did not identify 'the Church' with the Church of Rome, but said the Church "subsists in" (*subsistere*) the Roman Catholic Church. Presbyterianism has never disenfranchised Roman Catholicism as a Church, although rejecting dogmas like Papal infallibility and transubstantiation. While sincerely asserting with John Knox's words about the Reformed Church in Geneva that:

This place... is the maist perfyt schoole of Chryst that ever was in the erth since the dayis of the Apostillis...

presbyterianism sees the Church of Rome as a part of the body of Christ.

Even in Ireland, with the exception of obscurantists, the use of abusive language has for the most part disappeared. And that is saying something.

Vatican II set forth a new ecclesiology, especially in its placing the hierarchy within the people of God, its concept of collegiality, and its emphasis upon participation of the laity. Let us remember that 'the Church is the people of God' so we must not overlook the fact that it was Christians who helped found Corrymeela, Glencree, PACE, Nimma, All Women Together and many organisations of similar outlook. All are part of the ecumenical movement. In many areas groups meet for joint Bible-study, councils of churches, conferences and meetings for prayer. Today, we engage at the highest level.

The Reformed Churches of Europe and Britain, including the Irish Presbyterian Church, at a Conference in Vienna in 1969, concluded that:

The changes (*aggiornamento*) taking place inside the Roman Catholic Church do not signify a Reformation, neither are they taking place according to one overall pattern. Reformed minority Churches should be aware of the dangerous ambiguity which can be brought about by these renewals in situations where the Roman Catholic Church is almost absolute. On the other hand Roman Catholicism is visibly changing... They open the door to what could be a fruitful dialogue with the Reformed Churches. Dialogue with the Roman Catholic Church is for the reformed Churches a necessary task.

This is the standpoint of World presbyterianism. Unfortunately, I regret that I cannot say that this is accepted by all members of the General Assembly. Nevertheless, there has been progress in spite of many frustrations (*progressus ex variis frustrationibus*). I know I am only a very small fish in a very large pool — but a very small fish can cause a ripple. What did I accomplish? Viewing it as objectively as is possible, I think I helped Irish Roman Catholicism to understand and respect presbyterianism. On the other hand, I think I failed to help Irish presbyterianism, except for a few individuals, to grasp fully the 'openness' created within Roman Catholicism by Vatican II. While I tried, perhaps history shows that only a Roman Catholic can do this, though that does not excuse my failure. Let me hope that by God's grace, I at least tilled the ground.

It is useless to attempt to deny that recently there has been a cooling off so far as ecumenism is concerned. Many of John Paul II's views are reactionary. There has been a retreat in moral thinking. There is the Instruction on the Ecclesiological Vocation of the Theologian (I reject its claims without equivocation). There has been the silencing of theologians. The Presbyterian Church in Ireland was a member of the WCC, BCC, and ICC from their foundation, but have withdrawn from the WCC in 1980, from the Tripartite Negotiations in 1988, and refused to join the Council of Churches in Britain and Ireland in 1989. I cannot say that I am proud of these decisions as there is no doubt in my mind that the General Assembly has departed from the theological tradition and ethos of the Reformed Church as it is set out in The Proceedings of the World Alliance of Reformed Churches in 1948 and 1964. All appear to be retiring to their polemical trenches.

This calls for a final comment. The Renaissance sought the recovery of a past golden age, whereas the Reformation was a creative movement. There are sections of Protestantism today which are still preoccupied with fighting old battles. The Papacy is still intent on upholding paternalist authoritarianism. The Irish Churches, Catholic and Protestant, are so captive to cultural traditions they are unable to provide the transcendence which can lead, under God, to the transformation of all cultural traditions. But the ecumenical journey into unity will continue. It means too much to too many to end here.

I have been denounced as a Jesuit and a Judas Iscariot for the stand I have taken. While others might perhaps have followed different lines of approach, all I can say is that at all times I have tried to be faithful to Christ as Lord and to presbyterianism as a Church-Order that is 'holy' (*hagios*, not *hosios*), 'Catholic' (*oikoumene, katholiken*), and '*apostolic*' (aposoliken). I rest my case.

10 Opening the field

I presided as Principal at the closing Public Meeting of Union Theological College on Friday 29 May, 1981, and resigned to the General Assembly on 5 June, to take effect from 30 September following. Being in a tied house, most of the summer was taken up with moving, repairs, painting, mowing grass and cutting hedges.

I determined not to vegetate, and so during my first two years of retirement listed all the sixteenth and seventeenth century books in the College Library. As nothing had been done on the *Fasti* since 1840, I decided to bring it up to 1910. This is a continuous type of work so perhaps next year I will get time to add the material collected since then.

In May, 1985, I received an invitation from the Rev. S.J. Campbell, the Minister, to preach on 22 September in Cooke Centenary Church. I accepted immediately and without thinking; at the time, I looked on it as simply a matter of standing in for him while he conducted Harvest Thanksgiving services elsewhere. A while after, I had a letter from a friend saying how sorry he was that he would be unable to be present at my Golden Jubilee. Then it dawned on me. I must thank Mr. Campbell, his wife Ruth, and the Session and congregation. No effort was spared to make the Service of Thanksgiving and the reception a success. It was an unexpected honour for it was over thirty-one years since I had been minister of the congregation. Mr. Campbell read the Scriptures and led the prayers, the singing was led by the Ulster College of Music Madrigal Group (invited by Stephen Hamill the organist), and I preached. They sang my favourite metrical Psalm: *Now Israel may say, and that truly, If that the Lord had not our cause maintained...* There is nothing finer to my mind than a presbyterian congregation of six or seven hundred singing this psalm *forte* (not shouting) and then bursting forth *fortissiimo:*

> Therefore our help
> Is in the Lord's great name,
> Who heaven and earth
> By his great power did frame.

It is a link with my roots — Calvin opened every Service of public worship he ever conducted with the words "Our help is in the name of the Lord who made heaven and earth" (Ps.124.8). It is a battle-cry which saved many members of the Reformed faith from death in days of persecution — and remember my grandmother was a Huguenot. It also forms a link with my fellow-students who, each year, formed a guard of honour through which the professor had to pass on his way to the examination hall while we sang of "cruel men who us desired to slay". They also sang my favourite hymn from Bonar's *Hymns of faith and Hope:*

> Glory be to God the Father,
> Glory be to God the Son,
> Glory be to God the Spirit,
> Great Jehovah, Three in One!

As I have already remarked, like my father before me I was always tense before conducting a service and this was no exception. When I entered the Church to find the ground floor packed and even a number on the gallery, I felt such a wave of friendly-feeling sweep round me (it was almost physical and I believe it was God-given) that all my tension immediately disappeared. I don't think I ever felt more relaxed in my life.

At the reception afterwards, the hall was packed. I cannot name all who were present, but I feel it would be remiss not to refer to some. The Very Rev. Dr. A.J. Weir, Clerk of Assembly, and the Rev. Dr. R.D.E. Gallagher, former President of the Methodist Church, were there. I was pleased that Mrs Margaret Haire and my colleagues Professors E.A. Russell, J.S. M'Ivor, and John Thompson, and the two men who had been my assistants, Rev. Dr. W.D. Bailie and Rev. J.I. Davey, were present. Though they were unable to attend, the congratulations and good wishes from two distinguished former students, the Rev. W.A. McComish, D.D. (Geneva) and Mr. W.Ian P. Haslett, D.Theol. (Glasgow), gladdened my heart. Roman Catholics present included the Most Rev. Cahal B. Daly, Bishop of Down (now Primate), Most Rev. Mgr. Robert Murphy and Rev. Frs Hugh Murphy and Brendan Murray. Though this may appear a bit of a catalogue, there were two others I dare not omit. They are Dom. Placid Murray O.S.B. and Bro. Patrick Hederman O.S.B., who came the whole way from Glenstal to rejoice with me. Some thirty came from Drumreagh, my first congregation, including the Minister, the Rev. T. Luke, James Walker (the first child I had baptised), James Fulton, Session clerk, who along with several others, was a member of my first Bible Class in Balnamore. Several arrived from Ballybay, First Ballymacarrett and Belmont. Many from student days and of my co-presbyters were in the congregation. Lastly, there was a large attendance of Cooke and former Cooke members; and the congregation presented me with a beautiful line-drawing of the Church. Let me thank all.

These years also saw a complete change in my home life. Irene had been ill for over ten years. Now I had to take over most of the cooking and household chores as well as nursing. Eventually, there came a day when the latter became an impossibility. Something had to be done and she was admitted to Clifton House. With the help of Lois it was possible to ensure that when she was completely confined to bed she was visited daily. She died on 29 July 1987.

Some fifteen months later, I married my long-standing friend Carrie Barnett. She was brought up as a member of Ormond Quay and Scots Church, Dublin, but I had known her well since 1949 as she was at that time a member of Cooke.

In addition to being a churchman, I am a member of a number of organisations outwith the Church which mean a lot to me, such as Corrymeela, founded by the Rev.Dr. Ray Davey, a presbyterian minister, who was succeeded by another, the Rev.Dr. John Morrow. Its aim is to be a reconciling community, to be a place of hope where people who differ radically can meet and talk. I am also proud to be a member of PACE (Protestant and Catholic Encounter). Notice it is encounter, not confrontation. It too is the brainchild of a presbyterian minister, the Rev. Desmond E.K. Mock. Here I play a more active role, speaking and writing articles for the *PACE Journal.* I also periodically attend the Social Studies Conference, an independent, voluntary organisation whose aim is to contribute to the formation of an enlightened public opinion based on Christian principles. My lectures on 'Roots of Sectarianism' and 'On being Protestant in Ireland' have been published in its proceedings. Here one can always be sure of a friendly, critical, and objective approach.

Every Thursday I go down to the Strandtown Probus Club. When I was invited to become a member I thought it took its title from the Latin *probus* meaning 'honourable', 'virtuous', 'excellent', 'upright' but discovered it comes from 'Pro' for professional, and 'bus' for business. My fellow members are retired men from many walks of life. We drink our tea or coffee, tell our stories, and settle all the problems of mankind to our own satisfaction. After which we make our way homewards looking forward to the chat and cheer of the following week.

I am also a member of the Ancient Free and Accepted Masons of Ireland. Some may find this strange in a churchman, but I see no contradiction between being a Christian and being a Mason. Freemasonry is not a religion, or a substitute for a religion. It is a system of morals. I will leave it to others to defend Masonry against the false charge of being a secret society, or against the charge of Masonic discrimination in the field of appointments and jobs. All I can say is that in over forty years as a Mason only once was I ever canvassed to support a man because he was a Mason for an appointment. I freely admit it was once too many. I did not vote for him. He was breaking the Masonic instruction that integrity, merit and competence were the touchstones. Yet, ironically, as a minister, I regularly and willingly gave references for members of the congregation. One also hears quasi-sectarian accusations. However, as Charles Horton, the Order's archivist, reminds us:

the Order in Ireland was predominantly Catholic until after the 1840s when Daniel O'Connell, the Liberator, resigned from the Order after being informed that membership of the Order and the Roman Catholic Church was incompatible.

O'Connell described the Order as "Philanthropy unconfined by sect, nation, colour, or religion". I agree with him, and like my father before me and my Uncle John, after whom I was called, I am proud to be a Mason.

The year 1990 was the one hundred and fiftieth anniversary of the formation of the General Assembly of the Presbyterian Church in Ireland. It was marked by the holding of a Special Assembly at Coleraine, in an effort to heal the present division within the Church. I hope and trust it will prove successful, so I will make no comment, except to say that there did appear to be a more generous spirit during its meetings than had been felt during the first week of June for about fifteen years. Some people have been as eulogistic about Coleraine as the panegyrics on Constantine of Eusebius of Caesarea. I think this is mistaken. You may ask: 'Why, in view of your hope, do you say this?' The reason is that it did not get down to the nitty-gritty. Basic issues remain unconfronted, for example, the authority of Church courts, the limits of ecclesiastical law, the parity of ministers, the difference between claim and fact in the Church's power to determine her doctrine, the right of a minister to close his pulpit against a brother, the right to deny those legally elected installation to office, and others.

I have also had my own commemoration, and that of an event of almost comparable antiquity. On my eightieth birthday, I was taken out to dinner in the Quarry Inn at Dundonald, by two delightful people — Lois, with her relaxed attitude to life, her loving and caring spirit towards everyone, and her great sense of humour; and Carrie, more serious with her Dublin wit, so different from that of North Antrim, her thoughtfulness for all sorts of people and the ability to uplift and encourage. It was an evening of happiness and joy.

God has been very good to me in that I have always enjoyed good health. So, even when I retired, I just ploughed on. Since joining the National Health Service, I have had three doctors. The first and second I never had to call on. I do not think I troubled the third until 1985, after I got a foundering in a snowstorm at Limburg. However, after a couple of weeks I recovered and went on my way as if I was forty. But about a fortnight after my eightieth birthday, I found myself in hospital. I think I was probably as near to kicking the bucket as ever I will be until I eventually do so. I owe a lot to my doctor, the consultant, and the Angels of 'The Ulster' and I do not mean *Ireland's Saturday Night*. They were wonderful and could fill even me (always a bad riser) with cheer at 6.30 am.

During that fortnight, I thought about many things. I reflected that, amongst the few people who will come out of the present troubles with untarnished honour will be the medical profession - doctors, surgeons, nurses, hospital staff. The Churches have exercised an excellent pastoral ministry to the bereaved, the sick, the intimidated, the widow and the orphan. But they have failed to provide leadership. In days gone by the Synod of Ulster issued an annual address to the people. This is no longer done. Communication and leadership have to a significant extent broken down. Reports such as the Assembly's 'Report on Discrimination' which won applause in the *Irish News* in 1967 mean nothing if people do not live up to them in their daily lives.

I also thought about how, in a lecture in 1974, I described the troubles as an *internal* problem — that is, deriving from the relations between the two communities in Northern Ireland — with an *external* element, in that London and Dublin were both politically involved. I held that if the former was resolved the latter would follow as both London and Dublin would be dealing with a united people. Then there could be a harmonious evolution.

You could make an analogy with the USA. The American War of Independence did not establish a British/American relationship, but thirteen Britain-state relationships. The only body on which all thirteen States were represented was the Presbyterian Synod. It was the model on which American government was founded. The question is: are the Churches in Ireland equipped to provide a similar example? They were not in 1969 They may be today. All the historic Churches in Ireland are churches of the whole island, and have an interest in its welfare, north and south. All have world links, which should widen parochial perspectives. We have at long last put in place the mechanisms which allow us to talk to one-another. Let us now use them to the full.

Of course, there is one blot on this pleasing horizon. Anglicans, Methodists and Roman Catholics meet as members, or observers in the Council of Churches for Britain and Ireland (CCBI) but without the presence of Irish presbyterianism. The General Assembly rejected participation by 453 votes to 289 in 1989, with about 100 recording dissent — including myself. Sadly, the Presbyterian Church has now no voice in its proceedings. I deplore the fact that those who could have co-operated and worked for reconciliation can only do so now as individuals.

Fourthly, I thought of fundamentalism, of its rise in Islam and how, in Christian thought, it has resulted in ultramontanism and exclusivism reviving Catholic-Gaelicism and Orange-Toryism, with their *Jihad* mentalities. Unless Protestants and Roman Catholics completely change their attitudes to one-another all political agreements are doomed to failure. What is most needed is a complete change of heart. This will not come out of nothing. Our social and educational structures must first be radically overhauled. I pray that God may grant us grace and healing.

Finally, I remembered how at harvest time my Uncle Johnny would put a stone in his shirt pocket and a scythe over his shoulder and take me to the corn-field, to "open the field" for the reaper to cut the corn. We would cut a few swathes and then go. In a way this seems a lot like my own life. Perhaps my God-given task was to open the field for the reaper, not to reap. May the harvest of Christian brotherhood in Ireland yet be won.

Let me conclude. I was born within God's Covenant and my spiritual home is within presbyterianism. I firmly agree with Professor John 'Rabbi' Duncan who, when asked what he was replied: "I am first a Christian, secondly a Catholic, thirdly a Calvinist, fourthly a Paedo-Baptist (infant baptism), and fifthly a presbyterian." I agree. The first four are essentials to being presbyterian. One cannot be truly presbyterian if he or she is not obedient to Christ; if he or she is not Catholic, believing that the Church of Christ is one and that she should be seen to be one; if he or she is not Calvinist, accepting the sovereignty and rule of God in Christ over the whole of life; and if he or she does not believe the children of believers are within God's Covenant and should be received into the membership of God's family. These are essentials to being truly presbyterian. I have tried to live and, by my life and actions, to witness to these truths.

Whether I have been sufficiently faithful also to be described as a Dissenter and Blackmouth is not for me but for my readers to judge.

I set out the inspiration of my life in the words of Kate Compton's poem, *Christchild:*

> So this is God's Word:
> not a principle, nor a code of ethics,
> not another neat ideology,
> nor an eloquent philosophy,
> but a little child...
> stabbing us to new awareness,
> beckoning us to new life.
>
> Father, bring us down from our pedestals,
> our pronouncements,
> our dogmas,
> which so often we worship
> in place of the living Christ...
> Bring us down from the pride
> of our certainties
> our arrogant sifting of everything
> into black and white...
> Shock us again with the scandal
> of the baby, the powerless child,
> who questions our pretensions...
> Bring us down to earth, God...
> in childlike wonder...

Ireland, showing some of the places mentioned in the text.

Appendix A: reasons for dissent

The right of the Presbyterian Church in Ireland to determine her own doctrine is not at present recognised in law in either part of Ireland. In 1973 the Assembly abandoned approaching both the Westminster and Dublin parliaments to have this right which she has always claimed recognised. As I believed, and believe, this recognition to be of profound importance, I recorded my dissent (see chapter 8). The full text can be read in the minutes of the General Assembly of June 8, 1973.

These reasons and authorities have never been answered.

I, John Monteith Barkley, while recognising that the Judicial Commission, in the light of Presbytery replies, were compelled to bring in this Report, do hereby record my dissent to the General Assembly of the Presbyterian Church in Ireland, simply receiving that section of the Report stating that "The Commission should not take any further steps in the matter", and consequently refusing to take the action necessary to ensure that the inherent rights of the Church are recognised in Law.

In accordance, therefore, with the Common Law of Presbyterianism, which required that if I state my reasons I must quote my authorities, I set out my reasons for dissent:

1. Because it is contrary to the teaching of Jesus Christ, the only King and Head of the Church, to allow that the civil magistrate may determine the doctrine, worship and government of His Church.
   (St. Mark 1, 22; 8, 33; 12,13-17; 15, 2; St. Matthew 4, 1-11; 10, 18; 21, 23-27; 22, 15-22; 28, 18; St. Luke 4, 1-13; 11, 20; 20, 20-36; 23, 1-3; St. John 6, 15; 10, 17-18; 17, 13-26; 18, 33-36; 19, 19; etc.).

2. Because it is contrary to the teaching of the Apostolic Church to allow that the civil magistrate may determine the doctrine, worship and government of the Church of Christ.
   (Acts 1, 7-8; 5, 29; 13, 26-30; 18, 33-37; Romans 13, 1-8; with 1 Cor. 2, 8; 6, 1-8; 12, 1-18; 15, 25; Phil. 2, 10-11; Col. 1, 17-19; 2, 15; Heb. 10, 13; Rev. 11, 15; 20, 10-15; etc.).

3. Because it is contrary to the doctrine of the Fathers and early Councils to allow that the civil magistrate may determine the doctrine, worship and government of the Church of Christ.
   (Cyprian, *de Unitate Catholicae Ecclesiae*; Athanasius, *contra Arianos* 32-33, 44; Basil, *Epistolae* 225; 286; 289; Lucifer of Cagliari, *pro. S. Athanasio* 1; Hilary, *ad Constantium* 1; Chrysostom, *ad Theodosium* 1; Ambrose, *Epistolae* 21, 2, 4, 17; 40; 41; *Sermo contra Auxentium*; Augustine, *de*

Civitate Dei 19, 15-17; Gelasius, *ad Anastasium*; etc.
Council of Antioch (341), canons 4, 11, 12; Council of Constantinople
(381), can. 6; Council of Chalcedon (451), sess. 1; Council of Paris (557),
can. 8; etc.).

4. Because it is contrary to the doctrine of the mediaeval Fathers to allow that
   the civil magistrate may determine the doctrine, worship and government of
   the Church of Christ.
   (John Damascene, *Orationes* 1; 2; Gregory II, *Epistolae* 12; 13; Humbert,
   Libri III adversus Simoniacos; Ivo of Chartres, *Epistola ad Hugonem
   Archiepiscopum-Lugundesum*; Bernard of Clairvaux, *de Consideratione* pp.
   11, 17-18, 56-58, 119-121; Hugh of St. Victor, *de Sacramentis Christianae
   Fidei*; John of Salisbury, *Policroticus* 4, 2-4; Gratian, *Decretum Distinctiones*
   22 c.l.; CJC 1.73; Thomas Aquinas, *Summa Theologia* I-II q.91; *de Regimine
   Principum, Commentum in IV Libros Sententarium*; John of Paris, *de
   Potestate Regia at Papali*; John Wyclif, *de Potestate Papae*; *de Officio
   Regis*; *de Ecclesia*; *Magna Carta Hiberniae* c.1; Statute of Kilkenny cc.1,
   8, 9; etc.).

5. Because it is contrary to the doctrine of the Reformers to allow that the
   civil magistrate may determine the doctrine, worship and government of the
   Church of Christ.
   (Luther, On the Councils and the Church; On the Secular Authority; Romans
   13. 1-8 WA 56. 16-20, 123-124; 50. 509-653; *Melancthon, Loci Communes
   Theologici*, edit. Pauck pp. 148-150; Bucer, *de Regno Christi* 1. 2; Bullinger,
   Of the Holy Catholic Church, edit. Bromley pp. 321-324; Decades 2. 7; 5.
   1; Calvin, *Institutes* IV. 8. 1, 2, 8, 9, 13; IV. II. 1-16; IV. 20. 2, 5, 9, 15, 22;
   CR 13. 72; 24. 357; 29. 532-533, 553; 37. 211; 41. 377; 43. 135, 139; 52.
   266-267, 426; 53. 135, 143; Knox, *Works*, edit. Laing II. 186-188, 195,
   202-203, 205-206, 225-226, 228, 230, 235-237, 241, 245-246, 254; IV.
   294; etc.).

6. Because it is contrary to the doctrine of Presbyterianism to allow that the
   civil magistrate may determine the doctrine, worship and government of the
   Church of Christ; for while all Reformed Confessions recognise the authority
   of the civil powers and inculcate obedience 'in so far as nothing contrary to
   God is commanded' and 'so long as they are acting in their own sphere'
   none gives the civil magistrate (or any organisation outwith the Church)
   any authority in the Church in matters of doctrine, worship and government.
   (*Tetrapolitan Confession* 15, 23; *I Confession of Basle* 5, 8; *I Helvetic
   Confession* 14, 16, 26; *Lausanne Articles* 8; *Genevan Confession* 18, 21;
   Gallican Confession 27-31, 39-40; *Scots Confession* 16, 18, 24; *Belgic
   Confession* 27, 30, 36; II *Helvetic Confession* 17-18, 30; *Lebendiges
   Bekenntnis* 1; *Barmen Declaration* 5; Confession of 1967 pref.; etc.
   Act of 1647 of Church of Scotland; Great Ejectment, 1662; Exeter Assembly,

1691; Act of 1729 of Presbyterian Church USA; etc).

7. Because it is contrary to the doctrine and practice of the Church of Scotland to allow that the civil magistrate may determine the doctrine, worship and government of the Church of Christ.
(Acts of Scottish Parliament 1567, 1581, 1592; Andrew Melville to James IV; Protests of 1637; National Covenant of 1638; Glasgow Assembly, 1638; Disruption of 1843; Church of Scotland Act 1921; Act of Union, 1929; *Practice and Procedure in the Church of Scotland* ed. Longmuir pp1-17; etc.).

8. Because it is contrary to what has always been the doctrine and practice of Irish presbyterianism to allow that the civil magistrate may determine the doctrine, worship and government of the Church of Christ.
(Presbytery of Ulster, 1646; *Complaint to Commissioners* by Stewart and McNeill, 1646; Ejectment, 1662; Presbyterian Committee, 1670; Synod of Ulster, 1803; General Assembly 1843; Membership and voters in Church Courts in Codes, 1825, 1841, 1859, 1868, 1887, 1912, 1948, 1962; Codes 1825, 1841, i. 2; 1859, 1868, 1887 para. 6; 1912, 1848, 1962 para. 7.).

9. Because it is contrary to the doctrine in the Rule of Faith of the Presbyterian Church in Ireland to allow that the civil magistrate may determine the doctrine, worship and government of the Church of Christ.
(Chapter ii of *The Code,* 1859, 1868, 1887, 1912, 1948, 1962).

10 Because the Reverend the General Assembly instructed a Commission to obtain Opinion of learned Counsel, which was that the inherent right of the Church to determine her doctrine, worship and government is not "recognised in law", to refuse to take the action necessary to establish and secure the Crown Rights of the Redeemer in His Church is, in my opinion, to be unfaithful to a fundamental doctrine of the Reformed Church.
(Assembly Minutes, 1969-72; Assembly Reports, 1970-72; Opinion of Counsel; Minutes of Judicial Commission, 1969-71; etc.).

11 Because I was baptised within, received my Christian nuture within, and was brought to a saving knowledge as Saviour and Lord within the Presbyterian Church in Ireland, whose inherent right as a Church of Christ, "distinct from the civil magistracy", to determine her doctrine, worship and government in my ordination vows I, in Christ's name, undertook to defend and maintain.
(*The Code,* 1912 paras. 7, 16-20, 368D (5), 338D (8), 338E; *The Code,* 1962 paras. 7, 16-20, 368D (5), 368D (8), 368E; Assembly Minutes, 1963;

John M. Barkley

Appendix B: complete bibliography

Books

Edit. *Handbook on Evangelical Christianity and Romanism,* compiled by Youth
  Committee of Presbyterian Church in Ireland (Belfast 1949)
Presbyterianism (Belfast 1951, revised 1966)
Edit. 'Service for St. Patrick's Day', 'Prayers from Irish Sources', and contributed
  prayer for St. Columba's Day in *Daily Service* (Northern Ireland edition),
  edit. G.W. Briggs Oxford 1951)
The Westminster Formularies in Irish Presbyterianism (Belfast 1956)
A Short History of the Presbyterian Church in Ireland (Belfast 1959)
The Sabbath School Society for Ireland (Belfast 1962)
The Eldership in Irish Presbyterianism (Belfast 1963)
Edit. *Book of Public Worship,* contributing prayers in Holy Communion,
  Licensing, and Ordination Services and for Reformation Sunday (Belfast
  1965; revised 1966)
The Presbyterian Orphan Society (Belfast 1966)
Worship of the Reformed Church (London 1966, Richmond 1967)
The Romeward Trend in Irish Presbyterianism? (Belfast 1968)
St. Enoch's Congregation, Belfast (Belfast 1972)
Edit. *Irish Psalter words and harmonised tunes* (Oxford 1975)
Edit. *Handbook To The Church Hymnary* (third edition), contributing 'The
  Revision' and biographical notes and notes on hymns and tunes (Oxford
  1979)
Edit. et al *Glenstal Liturgy* (Limerick 1986)
Edit. *Fasti of the Presbyterian Church in Ireland 1840-70* (Belfast 1986)
Edit. *Fasti of the Presbyterian Church in Ireland 1871-90* (Belfast 1987)
Edit. *Fasti of the Presbyterian Church in Ireland 1891-1910* (Belfast 1987)

Articles in Dictionaries

Articles on 'Nordirland' and 'Ireland Republik' in *Weltkirchenlexikon,* edit.
  F.H. Littell and H.H. Walz (Stuttgart 1960)
Articles on 'Baptism', 'Burial', and 'Ordination' in *A Dictionary of Liturgy
  and Worship,* edit. J.D. Davies (London 1972)
Article on 'Irish Metrical Psalters' in *New Grove Dictionary of Music and
  Musicians,* edit S. Sadie (London 1979)
Articles on 'Baptism', 'Burial', and 'Ordination' in A New Dictionary of Liturgy
  and Worship, edit. J.D. Davies (London 1986)

Pamphlets

The Baptism of Infants (Belfast 1963)
The Book of Public Worship: An Open Letter (Belfast 1965)
Public Worship: Presbyterian Forms (Belfast 1966)
The Anti-Christ (Belfast 1967)
Christian Unity: What is it? (Belfast 1970)
The Roman Catholic Church: a Handbook for Parents and Teachers (Belfast 1974)
Irish Presbyterianism and Inter-Church Relations (Belfast 1975)
The Orthodox Churches of the East (Belfast 1976)
Thomas Toye: Revivalist Preacher (Belfast 1978)
Francis Makemie: Father of American Presbyterianism (Belfast 1981)
The Irish Council of Churches (Belfast 1983)
Francis Hutcheson (1694-1746) — Professor of Moral Philosophy, Glasgow (Belfast 1985)
Ministry in Ecumenical Perspective with special reference to Presbyterianism (New York 1987)
Ireland in Perspective, 1989 (London 1989)

Articles in Books

'The Irish General Assembly' in *A History of General Assemblies*, edit. C.M. Drury (Philadelphia 1960)
'What is the church? A comment' in *Church and Eucharist*, edit. M. Hurley (Dublin 1966)
'Some Scottish Bishops and Ministers in the Irish Church, 1610-35' in *Reformation and Revolution*, edit. D.W.D. Shaw (Edinburgh 1967)
'Christian Initiation in Presbyterianism' in *Ecumenical Studies*, edit. M.Hurley (Dublin 1968)
'The Eucharist in Presbyterianism' in *Understanding the Eucharist*, edit. P. M'Goldrick (Dublin 1969)
'Anglican-Presbyterian Relations' in *Irish Anglicanism* 1869-1969 edit. M. Hurley (Dublin 1970)
'Towards a Theology of Ecumenism' in *Directions: Theology in a Changing World*, edit. H.F. Woodhouse (Dublin 1970)
'The Arian Schism in Ireland, 1830' in *Schism, Heresy, and Religious Protest*, edit. D. Baker (Cambridge 1972)
'Ecumenism and Sectarianism in Ireland' in Sectarianism: *Roads to Reconciliation*, edit. P. Burke (Dublin 1974)
'Bullinger's Appeal to the Fathers' in *Henry Bullinger, 1504-75* edit. W.M.S. West (Bristol 1975)

'The Presbyterian Church in Ireland and the Government of Ireland Act, 1920' in *Church, Society and Politics*, edit. D. Baker (Oxford 1975)
'The Renaissance of Public Worship in the Church of Scotland, 1865-1905' in *Renaissance and Renewal in Christian History*, edit. D. Baker (Oxford 1977)
'Other Denominations' in *Who are we? What do we believe?*, edit. A.S. Worrall (Belfast 1977)
'Pleading His eternal sacrifice', in *The Sacrifice of Praise* edit. B.D. Spinks (Rome 1981)
'The Presbyterian Church in Ireland' in *International Church Index (Doctrine)* edit. R.A. Facey (Plymouth 1981)
'The Presbyterian Minister in the Eighteenth Century', in *Challenge and Conflict*, edit. J.L.M. Haire (Belfast 1981)
'The Roots of Sectarianism in Ireland' in *Options for a New Ireland*, edit. S. Farren (Belfast 1982)
'On being protestant' in *Being Protestant in Ireland*, edit. A. M'Loone (Dublin 1985)
'Moderators of the Presbyterian Churches in Ireland from 1690' in *A New History of Ireland*, vol 9, edit. T.W. Moody, F.X. Martin, F.J. Byrne (Oxford 1982)
'Church Relations within Ireland, 1948-1990'; 'The General Assembly and Society', in *The General Assembly of the Presbyterian Church in Ireland*, 1840-1990, edit R.F.G. Holmes and R.B. Knox (Belfast 1990)

Articles in pamphlets

'Two Bodies in Christ' in *Governing without Consensus, a Critique*, edit. J.P. Darby (Belfast 1972)
'Christianity in Ireland' in *Tribalism or Christianity in Ireland*, edit. A.S. Worrall (Belfast 1973)
'Salvation, Dialogue and Evangelism' in *The Presbyterian Church in Ireland and the World Council of Churches* (Belfast 1976)
'Do myths influence people?' in *Irish History: Fact or Fiction?*, edit. W.J.N. Mackey (Belfast 1976)

Articles in journals and press

Familia, Belfast: Late 18th Century Belfast and St.Mary's, Chapel Lane, 1784-1831; 1986
Church Service Society Annual, Edinburgh:
Old Irish Session Books, 1952; The Liturgical Movement and Reformed Worship, 1961
The Liturgical Review, Edinburgh: The Reformed Rite in Hungary, 1965; The Theology of Liturgy, 1972

Scottish Journal of Theology, Edinburgh: The Meaning of Ordination, 1956; 'Episcopate' and 'Presbyterate' in the Anglican Ordinal, 1958

The Furrow, Dublin: Baptism, Eucharist, Marriage, 1974

The Month, London: Presbyterian/Roman-Catholic Relations in Ireland, 1780-1965, 1981

Doctrine and Life, Dublin: cf. The Month, 1981 Comment on the Ecumenical Directory, part one, 1967

Verbum Caro: Taize: *La signification de l'ordination*, 1957

The Newman, London: Pope, Bishops and Church, 1969

The Newman Review, Belfast: Catholics through Protestant eyes (2 Parts), 1963

The Journal of Ecumenical Studies, Philadelphia: The 1967 Glenstal Ecumenical Congress, 1968

The Journal of Presbyterian History, Philadelphia: The Presbyterian Church in Ireland (2 Parts), 1960-67

Bulletin of the Presbyterian Historical Society, Belfast: Irish Presbyterian Magazines, 1829-40, 1970; Irish Non-Subscribing Presbyterian Magazines, 1972; Josias Welsh of Templepatrick, 1972; John Knox, minister of God's Word in Scotland, 1973; Irish Presbyterian Periodicals, 1840-1974, 1974; The Overseas Missionary Magazines of the Irish Presbyterian Church, 1977

The Christian Irishman, Belfast: Presbyterian Periodicals in connection with the Irish Mission, 1966

Biblical Theology, Belfast: The Historical and Doctrinal Basis of Public Worship, 1955; The Rule of Faith, 1956; The Proposed Scheme for the Ordination of Assistants, 1959 Deaconesses or Church Sisters, 1965; The Quest for Oneness, 1968; The Theology of the Child, 1973

Irish Biblical Studies, Belfast: Luther Quincentenary: The Significance of Luther for today, 1983

The Teacher's Guide, Belfast: The Sabbath School Society for Ireland, 1961

The Presbyterian Herald, Belfast: The Revival of 1859, 1959; The Reformation in Scotland, 1960; Union Theological College, 1978; Presbyterian/Roman Catholic Relations in Ireland (3 Parts), 1980; St. Patrick, 1987; St.Columba, 1988; *Ardens sed Virens*, 1988

The Donegal Annual, Ballyshannon: Francis Makemie, Founder of American Presbyterianism, 1984

The Church of Ireland Magazine, Dublin: Christian Unity, 1967

The Capuchin Annual, Dublin: Church and World, 1968

Focus, Dublin: Apostolic Succession: a Presbyterian view, 1958; The Way to Unity, 1965

Manse News, Edinburgh: cf Focus 1958, 1959

Faith and Unity, London: cf Focus 1965, 1965

Whitefriars, Dublin: The Road to Unity, 1971

New Ireland Journal, Belfast: St. Columba of Derry, 1964

Q. Review, Belfast: The Orange Order in Religion and Politics, 1962

PACE Journal, Belfast: One Hundred Years ago, 1971; Belfast Newspapers (7 Parts.), 1973-76; Irish Presbyterianism, 1920-22, 1973; The Irish Council of Churches and the Roman Catholic Church, 1974; To America by *Eagle Wing*, 1976; The American Declaration of Independence, 1976; Who crucified Christ? (5 Parts.), 1977-80; Father Michael Hurley, S.J. 1980; Calvin and Social Reform, 1982; Columbanus Community and Reconciliation, 1982; Dr. Wilberforce Arnold, 1983; John Edgar, social reformer, 1984; Two Derry Churches, 1984; Churchmens' Visit to Germany, 1986; The Moravian Tradition, 1988; The Cologne Declaration, 1989; Creeds, 1989; Obituary: Tomás Cardinal O'Fiaich, 1990

Belfast Telegraph, The Smaller Denominations (2 Parts.) 1958; The 1859 Revival, 1959; Causerie (8 Parts.), 1960; Martin Luther (2 Parts.), 1967; Education in Northern Ireland, 1970

Chronology

Born October 16, 1910

Baptised January 11, 1911

Received as a student (Derry Presbytery) 1930

Licensed 1935

Married Irene Graham 1936

Ordained in Drumreagh, Co. Antrim, 1935

Installed in Second Ballybay, Co. Monaghan, and appointed in charge of Rockcorry 1939

Adopted Lois 1943

Installed in Rockcorry 1947

Installed in Cooke Centenary, Belfast, 1949

Appointed Professor of Church History 1954

Installed in the Presbyterian College 1954 (now Union Theological College)

Appointed Principal of Presbyterian College 1976

Nominated for Moderatorship 1977

Retired 1981

Married Carrie Barnett 1988

Abbreviations

ICC	Irish Council of Churches
BCC	British Council of Churches
WCC	World Council of Churches
WPA	World Presbyterian Alliance
WARC	World Alliance of Reformed Churches
KEK	Council of European Churches
CCBI	Council of Churches of Britain and Ireland
IICM	Irish Inter-Church Meeting
MCD	Magee College, Derry
ACB	Assembly's College, Belfast
TCD	Trinity College, Dublin
QUB	Queen's University, Belfast
OUP	Official Unionist Party
DUP	Democratic Unionist Party
UUUP	United Ulster Unionist Party
SDLP	Social Democratic and Labour Party

Also available from the White Row Press:

Two Centuries of Life in Down 1600-1800
John Stevenson
Pbk, 508pp, illustrated, £7.95

Pirates roaming the coast, clerics being paid in beer, shopkeepers issuing their own coinage, French and Spanish money in daily circulation, hanging a man for stealing a chisel ... the County Down of several centuries age reads more like something from the world of science fiction than the place we are familiar with today.

In **Two Centuries of Life in Down 1600-1800**, John Stevenson seeks to bring this forgotten world to life, familiarising us with its customs, tastes and values, and subtly drawing the reader into the lives of a wide variety of its people, from the drunken Viscount and the dowager with servant trouble, to the small farmer facing eviction.

No subject is too trivial for him. He is as happy discussing fashion, witchcraft, hospitality and folk cures, as the Kirk, Public Morals, or the dangers of reading Milton. The result is something of a *tour de force*, a book of vast range and daring, and one of the great landmarks of literary County Down.

"no dry-as-dust academic work this, but a wonderful source for local historians, and a marvellous read for anyone who is interested in County Down ..."
W. A. Maguire. Keeper of Local History, Ulster Museum.

The Most Unpretending of Places
A History of Dundonald, County Down
Pbk, 256pp, illustrated, £7.95

"Sparkles with compelling detail .... one of the most impressive local histories available for any locality on this island, north or south." *Linenhall Review*

"One word could suffice to describe this book, magnificent! ... I cannot praise it too highly. Well illustrated with photographs, studiously annotated without over-loading the text, a questioning of sources, a good index and the courage to express opinions of a controversial nature. This is what local history is all about." *Irish News*

Yes Matron
A history of nurses and nursing at the Royal Victoria Hospital, Belfast
Peggy Donaldson
Hbk, 200pp, illustrated, £12.50

Drawing both on her own nursing experience and a rich vein of oral and archive material, Peggy Donaldson creates a fresh and readable narrative that will delight, surprise and be treasured by anyone with an interest in nursing.

"Examines both great events and small, from the impact of wars and devastating epidemics, to the dramas of everyday hospital life ... a humorous, heartwarming, moving story." *Belfast Telegraph*

Gape Row
Agnes Romilly White's classic comedy set in a small Irish village on the eve of the First World War
Pbk, 200pp, £4.95

"Captures the spirit of early twentieth century rural Ulster better than any painter or photographer could." *Sunday News*

"masterly ... the dialogue goes to one's head like wine" *The Observer*

Available from most bookshops or directly from the publishers